Contents

1. Introduction 1

2. Form of Clandestine Cellular Networks 13

3. Function of Clandestine Cellular Networks 39

4. Logic of Clandestine Cellular Networks 61

5. The Principles of Clandestine Cellular Networks 69

6. Conclusion and Recommendations 73

7. Appendix A – Types of Clandestine Cellular Networks 81

8. Appendix B – Clandestine Potential 89

Endnotes 93

1. Introduction

Design of effective countermeasures depends on first understanding undergrounds.[11] — Andrew R. Molnar, et. al. (1963)

It's hard for us to fight the cells because they're many different leaders, different thought processes, it's not like a normal enemy we fight, it's not structured.[12] — U.S. Army Intelligence Officer, Iraq (2006)

I'm not sure we really understood how embedded Al Qaeda was becoming.... Al Qaeda in Iraq has proved to be a very resourceful enemy, capable of regenerating at a time when we thought it didn't have that capability.[13] — U.S. Army Battalion Commander, Iraq (2009)

Since the events of 11 September 2001, the United States military counternetwork operations, theory, and doctrine have failed to account for the form, function, and logic of clandestine cellular networks used by both interstate insurgencies, such as those in Iraq and Afghanistan, as well as by global insurgencies like al-Qaeda and its associated movements. The failure to understand the form, function, and logic of clandestine cellular networks has led to the incorrect application of counternetwork operations based on ill-informed counternetwork theories.[14] This monograph defines counternetwork operations as a subset of counterinsurgency and counterterrorism operations. Like counterguerrilla operations, counternetwork operations are focused on a specific element of the insurgency.[15] In this case, counternetwork operations are conducted against the clandestine cellular networks within an insurgency, specifically the underground and auxiliary, not the overt guerrilla elements. This is a counter organizational operational construct, not a strategy in-of-itself, as has happened with counterterrorism—a counter "tactic"—turned strategy. Although counternetwork operations are not specifically discussed in U.S. joint or service doctrine, since 9/11, these operations have been the primary offensive effort of both Special Operations and conventional forces, normally referred to as raids, direct-action, or intelligence-driven operations to capture or kill high-value individuals in the insurgencies in Iraq or Afghanistan, and globally against al-Qaeda and its associated movements. During this time, counternetwork operations have primarily focused on targeting key leaders, facilitators, individuals with special skills, or highly-connected individuals, all of which intuitively seem to be the correct targets for disconnecting clandestine cellular networks.[16] However, there has been little comparative analysis done to verify if these operations are in fact having the overall effect required to disrupt, neutralize, defeat, or ultimately destroy these networks.[17]

Understanding the form, function, and logic of clandestine cellular networks reveals that the removal of single individuals, regardless of function, is well within the tolerance of this type of organizational structure and thus has little long-term effect. Counternetwork operations focused on critical individuals, known as high-value individuals or targets (HVI or HVT), have not proven overly successful for this reason. They gain media attention, provide a momentary lift in the spirits of the counterinsurgent or counterterrorist effort, but rarely produce strategic effects as anticipated. A contemporary example of this was the death of Abu Musab Zarqawi (AMZ), the infamous al-Qaeda leader in Iraq, who was killed in 2006.[18] At the time, there was speculation that the death of Zarqawi would end the insurgency or at least seriously degrade the Sunni insurgency in Iraq.[19] However, it had little overall effect.[20] His organization was resilient enough that his deputy, Abu Ayyub al Masri (AAM), assumed his leadership role and continued to lead al-Qaeda in Iraq until AAM was himself finally killed in 2010.[21] With AAM's death, his replacement was quickly announced, and al-Qaeda in Iraq continued to conduct attacks in Iraq at the time of publication of this monograph.

At the same time, highly-connected individuals (HCI), or hubs, are another favorite target of counternetwork operations. However, these individuals violate the principles of clandestine operations since they and the connections to their associates are obviously highly visible when compared to a competent clandestine practitioner. The clandestine practitioner does not want a discernible link or signature with others in the network in order to remain hidden from the counterinsurgent. Thus, by focusing on the highly connected individuals as HVIs, U.S. and coalition efforts since 9/11 have effectively "culled the herd" of poor clandestine practitioners, while further educating the competent clandestine practitioners on U.S. and coalition counternetwork methods. This also allows other poor clandestine practitioners, those that may have been lucky enough to survive their incompetence, but were smart enough to learn from those not so fortunate, to adapt and increase their proficiency in the application of the clandestine arts.[22]

These two examples, high-value individuals and highly-connected individuals, provide the two most common types of errors in the current counternetwork theories and operations. These errors are all due to a lack of a systemic understanding of clandestine cellular networks and ultimately have a negative effect on the success of ill-informed counternetwork operations. Counternetwork methodologies, such as those described above, focused on kill or capture of HVIs or HCIs, are largely based on theories that clandestine cellular networks are social networks. Thus, the driving force behind the HVI and HCI counternetwork operational concepts are based on academically-driven social network analysis and theories that social networks can be defeated by removing key nodes to delink the network.[23] What emerged with the events of 9/11 and has now become readily accepted by counternetwork theorists and practitioners alike is the idea that the clandestine cellular networks used by adversaries like al-Qaeda and the insurgents in Iraq and Afghanistan, are "information-age networks."[24] Theorists describe these adversary networks as highly connected, flat, leaderless, agile, and adaptive, mirroring today's business networks or social networks like those found on the Internet.[25] Mark Buchanan, author of *Nexus*, explains, "Since the attacks, we have become accustomed to the idea that the West is battling against a decentralized 'network of terrorists cells' [sic] that lacks any hierarchical command structure and are distributed throughout the world. This network seems to be a human analogue of the Internet, with an organic structure that makes it extremely difficult to attack."[26]

However, as this monograph will show, clandestine cellular networks are not information-age networks, and despite the West's desire to mirror-image information-age networks onto insurgent and terrorist networks, the form, function, and logic of clandestine cellular networks are very different.[27] Clandestine cellular networks provide a means of survival in form through their cellular or compartmentalized structure, and in function through the use of clandestine arts or tradecraft to minimize the signature of the organization—all based on the logic that the primary concern is that the movement needs to survive to attain its political goals. The old adage that the insurgent wins by not losing is the fundamental driving force behind why insurgencies use this type of organizational structure, and why any organization conducting nefarious activities that could lead to being killed or captured by a government's security forces would use a similar structure.

Organizational structure, in this case clandestine cellular networks, and how they are established, grow, and operate, as well as the logic behind the organizational structure, plays a large role in the overall success of an insurgency.[28] Yet the importance of organization as a dynamic of insurgency is often overlooked or misunderstood by counterinsurgent theorists and practitioners. This is especially true when it comes to clandestine cellular networks.[29] Current counterinsurgency doctrine found in the Army's Field Manual (FM) 3-24, *Counterinsurgency*, provides only one dedicated paragraph on the role and "interplay" of organization in insurgency and one paragraph on clandestine networks.[30] Joint Publication (JP) 3-24, *Counterinsurgency Operations*, is only slightly better, with four pages on organization and one paragraph dedicated to networks.[31] However, both FM 3-24 and JP 3-24 use the same description, noting that clandestine networks "have a limited ability to attain strategic success because they cannot easily muster and focus power. The best outcome they can expect is to create a security vacuum leading to a collapse of the targeted regime's will and then to gain in the competition for the spoils."[32] Although neither manual backs up this statement with evidence, it is apparent that since 9/11 and in most historical cases of insurgency the underground and auxiliary members extensively used clandestine cellular networks as their organizational method to protect their core leadership, intelligence, logistics support, and some lethal operational capabilities.[33] For insurgents in hostile or non-permissive environments where there is a large government security presence or an unsympathetic population, especially in urban areas, clandestine cellular networks become the primary organizational structure.[34]

The lack of coverage of clandestine cellular networks in FM 3-24 and JP 3-24 is a great example of doctrinal concepts that fail to adequately describe and provide the reader an understanding of the enemy, even though the U.S. and the West have been involved in continuous counterinsurgency since 9/11, not to mention the other historical examples of U.S. counterinsurgency in Vietnam, Greece, and the Philippines to name only a few. As the operational basis for counterinsurgency operations, the lack of understanding of the clandestine cellular networks that make up the underground of an insurgency leads the counterinsurgent and ultimately the counternetwork practitioners astray. Instead of focusing the majority of the effort against the underground, the doctrine disproportionally focuses on the overt arm of the insurgency, the guerrilla. U.S. counterinsurgency operations and doctrine have always tended to focus on guerrillas since they are the overt military element of the insurgency, and more understandable from a military point of view. However, the guerrillas are the most expendable element of an insurgency because they are easily recuperated. This should be the first indicator of the lack of importance of these elements to the overall insurgent effort.[35]

The underground and auxiliary and their use of clandestine cellular networks have never been completely understood, and have always been minimized in their role in insurgency because they remained hidden. However, as the diagram in Figure 1 shows, historically, the overt guerrilla elements only make up the tip of the proverbial insurgency iceberg when compared to the underground and auxiliary.[36] In much the same way, a conventional military's ground forces have a disproportionate number of combat forces to noncombat forces, often referred to as the "tooth-to-tail ratio."[37] For the U.S. military, this ratio is generally 1:4, combat to noncombat troops, with the combat forces at the tip.[38] Based on the data presented in Figure 1, the average ratio is one guerrilla for every nine underground and auxiliary members.[39] Like conventional military organizations, insurgent organizations require significant non-combat support, including command and control, intelligence, logistics, and information, to support the overt combat elements of an insurgency. Thus, the statement from FM 3-24 and JP 3-24 that networks are unable to "muster and focus combat power," is wholly incorrect. The insurgents do not need, nor would they desire to focus combat power, since this would be counterproductive. In fact, the underground is not built to focus combat power; it is the antithesis of why the underground is organized in a clandestine and cellular form. The insurgents put themselves at risk even when they mass their guerrilla forces, and risk getting decisively engaged. Going back to the logic, the insurgent wins by not losing, so a long, drawn out series of seemingly minor attacks without decisive engagement erodes the will of their enemies. There is no need to "muster and focus combat power." Thus, doctrine fails to account for the asymmetry of insurgency. Insurgent warfare is not about combat power and decisive battles; it is about overall leveraging the lack of combat power to maintain pressure over time without being decisively engaged—the proverbial "death by a thousand cuts" or as counterinsurgency (COIN) expert Robert Taber

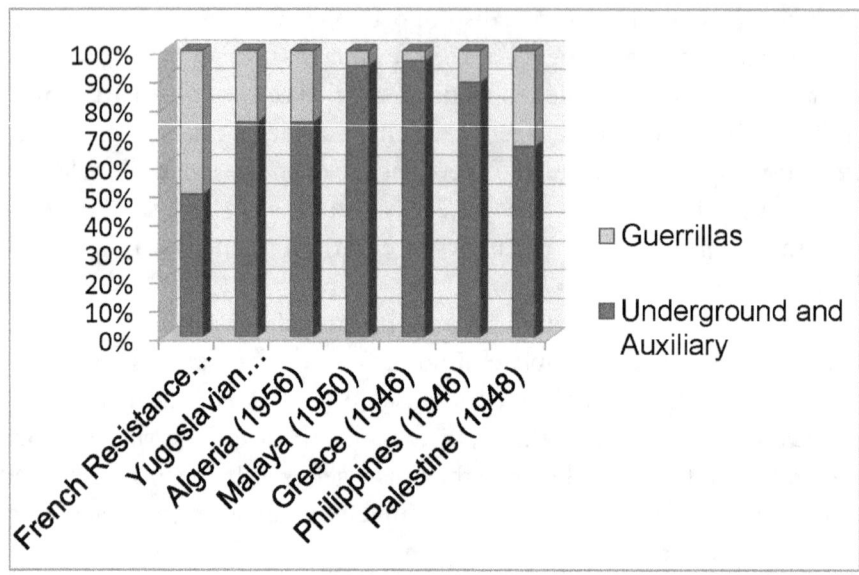

Figure 1. Historical Guerrilla to Underground and Auxiliary Ratios[40]

coined in 1965, the "war of the flea." [41] Understanding this fundamental paradox of insurgency begins to change the focus of counterinsurgency operations and ultimately counternetwork operations.

The insurgency in Iraq, which has been primarily an underground urban insurgency, is consistent with this idea. Every time the insurgents held ground or massed, such as in Fallujah, the conventional forces could generally deal them a decisive blow. Decisive in the sense that for a short time, they were defeated by massed conventional forces. On the other side of the coin, when insurgents were not identified and engaged decisively, the insurgents were able to leverage their asymmetric advantage by hiding within the population and striking on the insurgent's terms. Thus the coalition suffered casualties regularly from improvised explosive devices, small-arms fire from hit-and-run cells in urban areas, and snipers. It was these types of insurgent operations that successfully began to wear down U.S. public support and political will—arguably the U.S. center of gravity. It could also be argued that the Shi'a insurgency, with the external support of Iran, operated a generally clandestine insurgency that successfully stayed under the U.S. radar, except for overt Shi'a elements, like Muqtada al Sadr's Madhi Army. Iranian-backed Shi'a "Special Groups" operated as clandestine networks, and used explosively formed penetrators to inflict significant casualties on the coalition without the coalition forces being able to find a target to decisively engage after the attack.[42] Thus, failure to understand the form, function, and logic of clandestine cellular networks used by undergrounds and urban guerrillas has hampered U.S. counterinsurgency efforts.[43] With increased urbanization throughout the world, urban areas will become the primary environment of insurgency in the future, shifting away from rural-based insurgencies of the past. This shift in geography will set the stage for greater use of clandestine cellular networks in the future, and with it, an increasing need for counterinsurgency and counternetwork forces to fully understand clandestine cellular networks to ensure correct application of counternetwork operations.

Although Field Manual (FM) 3-24 fails to fully appreciate "organization" to an insurgency, the importance of organization has not been lost in the current or past Army Special Operations Forces (ARSOF) doctrine.[44] In the ARSOF Unconventional Warfare (UW) and Foreign Internal Defense doctrines, "organization" is one of the "seven dynamics of insurgency;" one of the analytical tools used by ARSOF for decades to understand insurgent movements.[45] The seven dynamics have been determined to be common to most insurgencies and, "provide a framework for analysis that can reveal the insurgency's strengths and weaknesses."[46] The other six dynamics are: leadership, ideology, objectives, environment and geography, external support, phasing and timing.[47] The 2006 FM 3-24 also uses "dynamics of insurgency," but has dropped organization, and thus only has six dynamics.[48] Although pieces and parts of the insurgent organization are discussed throughout the manual, the organizational role and importance is lost. Interestingly, Joint Publication (JP) 3-24 published three years later returns to the seven dynamics used by ARSOF, to include "organizational and operational approaches," and an additional dynamic, "internal support."[49] This is a positive step, but, as noted earlier, JP 3-24 fails to fully account for the importance of clandestine cellular networks.

Despite the lack of coverage in U.S. COIN doctrine, the importance of organization is readily apparent when reading past and highly respected COIN theorists such as Galula, Kitson, McCuen, Ney, Thompson, and Trinquier. All of these experts devoted numerous pages to describe the organization of an insurgency, including clandestine cellular networks, not just as parts, but the parts as the whole, and the whole within the context of the other dynamics of insurgency.[50] Trinquier went so far as to note, "In seeking a solution [to insurgency], it is essential to realize that in *modern warfare* we are not up against just a few armed bands spread across a given territory, but rather against an *armed clandestine organization*."[51] Trinquier further highlights, "Victory will be obtained only through the complete destruction of that organization. This is the master concept that must guide us in our study of *modern warfare*."[52]

The significance of organization has also not been lost on "modern" theorists. For example, famed insurgency and terrorism expert Bard E. O'Neill dedicates a chapter in his book *Insurgency & Terrorism* to the subject, while his contemporaries, noted experts Bruce Hoffman and John Arquilla have presented testimony to Congress on the organizational characteristic and function of al-Qaeda.[53] As O'Neill explains,

> No analysis of an insurgency will be complete or meaningful if it fails to address the scope, complexity, and cohesion of the insurgent movement. A careful look at the structures and workings of insurgent political and military organizations can reveal a good deal about the progress of an insurrection, as well as the type and magnitude of the threat confronting the government.[54]

Although it is apparent that the importance of "organization" was not lost on the COIN theorists of the past, the contemporary theorists' understanding of the form, function, and logic of clandestine cellular networks, minus the named few above, is less apparent or completely lacking.[55] Although theorists and practitioners regularly use phrases like "covert networks," "terrorist networks," and "undergrounds," they rarely codify what is meant by the description. In most cases, as will be shown in this work, they do not understand or they underestimate the significance of the terms, using them more as contemporary buzzwords than as technical terms.

Joint Publication 1-02 defines clandestine as, "Any activity or operation sponsored or conducted...with the intent to assure secrecy and concealment."[56] The 1960s-era Special Operations Research Office noted, "Clandestine operations are those whose existence is concealed, because the mere observation of them betrays their illegal and subversive nature. Secrecy depends upon the skill in hiding the operation and rendering it invisible."[57] Clandestine art or tradecraft is used to conceal individual actions, but also to conceal organizational functions, such as information and intelligence sharing, lethal and non-lethal operations, logistical support, and linkages to overt elements of the movement such as political wings or guerrillas.[58] "Clandestine," the adjective, describes the function of the network, while "cellular" describes the form or structure of the network. Both form and function help define the logic of these types of networks and the elements within the insurgencies that use them.

Reviewing historic works and documents on clandestine operations in insurgency and espionage, it becomes apparent that the form, function, and logic of clandestine cellular networks have largely remained unchanged.[59] Although some theorists might speculate that the information age caused a revolutionary change in clandestine networks, allowing for the rise of global non-state actors and thus an adaptation to clandestine networks' form, function, and logic, there is no evidence this has happened. Organizational use of clandestine cellular or compartmented networks (form) and the application of clandestine arts or tradecraft methods (function) have remained largely unchanged, having *evolved* to take advantage of the new technology, but not in a revolutionary way. Information technology, while increasing the rate and volume of information exchange, has also increased the risk to clandestine operations due to the increase in electronic and cyber signatures, which puts these types of communications at risk of detection by governments for example, like the U.S., who can apply their technological advantage to identify, monitor, track, and

> Information technology, while increasing the rate and volume of information exchange, has also increased the risk to clandestine operations...

exploit these signatures. Thus, despite the power of the Internet and other information-age electronic devices, clandestine operators continue to use old clandestine methods and, in some cases, adapt them for use with the new technology.[60] In fact, because they have to apply tradecraft, it slows their rate of communication down, thus denying the information-age theorists the monolithic, information-aged, networked enemy that they have portrayed since 9/11.

Another difference noted in clandestine literature is the scale of the different types of clandestine operations, from small networks of individuals conducting espionage, to insurgent movements utilizing clandestine cellular networks countrywide or globally. It is also interesting to note that based on the review of historical and current U.S., British, Soviet, Swiss, Iraqi, Iranian, and al-Qaeda clandestine tactics, techniques, procedures, and principles, there is a broad commonality amongst these different actors' clandestine theories and practices. The greatest difference is not in the operational application, since they all use almost identical methods, but surprisingly in vocabulary and professionalism. The bottom line is that clandestine cellular networks, regardless of the environment, the country of origin, the clandestine background of the practitioner, or the clandestine task—lethal operations, logistics, or intelligence gathering—they all generally have the same form, function, and logic.

Organization

The monograph is organized into four main sections—form, function, and logic, followed by the principles of clandestine operations that emerge from the previous three sections. Two additional appendixes provide further information, first on the specific types of clandestine networks—indigenous or external and professional or non-professional—likely to be encountered in a complex insurgency with multiple actors, and second, a description of the concept of the inherent "clandestine potential" of an indigenous population to provide a method for determining potential difficulties with future COIN and counternetwork operations as they relate to the clandestine organization of an insurgency.

This monograph will specifically focus on the organizational dynamic of insurgency to gain an understanding of the organizational form, function, and logic of insurgents' use of clandestine cellular networks. First, the *form* of clandestine networks will initially be explained with respect to how this organizational structure fits within the broader context of insurgency, then how these cellular networks are structured. The discussion on form will analyze the organizational structure, including size or scale, down to the cell level, and will focus on the key element of form for clandestine cellular networks—compartmentalization. Second, this work will explain how clandestine cellular networks *function* through the application of clandestine arts or tradecraft and reinforce the form of the organization, while most importantly explaining how insurgents use the clandestine arts or tradecraft to maintain a low signature. Lastly, the form and function will be synthesized to explain the *logic* behind the use of clandestine cellular networks by elements of insurgencies, both intrastate and global, which have an overall goal of ensuring the organization survives to reach its political goal. This final section will further explain the pressures faced by members of clandestine organizations. From this form, function, and logic analysis, a set of principles will be developed that capture the essence of clandestine cellular networks which can be used as a test of network theories.

2. Form of Clandestine Cellular Networks

One definition of form is "the shape or structure of something."[61] Clandestine elements of an insurgency use form—organization and structure—for compartmentalization, relying on the basic network building block, the compartmented cell, from which the term "cellular" is derived.[62] Structural compartmentalization at all levels ideally isolates breaches in security to a single cell, and even better, to a single individual. Cellular structure ensures that a single counternetwork strike does not lead to the compromise of the entire network, with only those individuals with direct linkages and knowledge to the detained individual being at risk. As Soviet defector Alexander Orlov explains, "the majority of the agents who take part in the same operation should not know one another, should not meet, and should not know each other's addresses. The idea behind [this] was, [sic] that if a man does not know something he will not be able to divulge it."[63] To understand the organizational significance of clandestine cellular networks, it is important to understand the context in which different components of the insurgency operate, the development and growth of clandestine cellular networks, elements of a clandestine cellular network, structural compartmentalization, scale of clandestine cellular networks, and finally, open and closed network structures.

Components of an Insurgency

The Army Special Operations Forces doctrine uses a three-component model of insurgency consisting of the underground, the auxiliary, and the guerrillas.[64] The underground and auxiliary are the primary components that utilize clandestine cellular networks, while the guerrillas are the overt action arm of the insurgency. First, the underground is responsible for the overall command, control, communications, information, subversion, intelligence, and covert direct action operations—such as terrorism, sabotage, and intimidation.[65] The original members and core of the insurgency generally operate as members of the underground. The underground cadres develop the organization, ideally building it from the start as a clandestine cellular network to ensure its secrecy, low-signature, and survivability. The underground members operate as the overarching leaders, leaders of the organization sub-networks and cells, training cadres, and/or subject matter experts for specialized skills, such as propaganda, explosive experts, or communications experts. These subject-matter experts train others and advise the underground leaders on operations. Some of the specialized skills may include specially trained and selected direct action elements that operate in direct control of the underground. These individuals may provide advanced demolitions or advanced weapons capabilities used for specialized operations that require compartmentalization and direct control of the underground leaders. Although these direct action cells are often confused with "urban guerrillas," they are different in that they are difficult to replace and rely on the clandestine cellular network to provide intelligence and close target reconnaissance, logistical support movement of specialized weapons into the target area, and then movement support to infiltrate the specialized direct action cells to the target, whereupon they synchronize the intelligence, specialized weapons, and their skills and training to interdict the target.[66] The network must then successfully move the direct action cell out of the target area safely and securely. Ultimately, the support network directed by the underground and described above makes up the second component, the auxiliary.

The auxiliary is the clandestine support personnel, directed by the underground which provides logistics, operational support, and intelligence collection to both the underground and the guerrillas.[67] The auxiliary members actively support the insurgency in most cases using their normal daily routines to provide them cover for their activities in support of the insurgency, to include freedom of movement, other specialized skills, or specialized capabilities for operations. The auxiliary members can enable the freedom of movement of other insurgent members by maintaining privileges for freedom of movement even if population control measures are in place. These individuals may hold jobs such as local security forces, shipping and ground transportation companies, doctors and nurses, and businessmen. These individuals' jobs provide them a plausible reason for the counterinsurgents to allow them to maintain their freedom of movement, even during a crisis. Thus the auxiliary members described above can clandestinely move other members of the insurgency, special packages, or messages without arousing suspicion of the counterinsurgents. Auxiliary members may also have specialized skills that provide the underground with critical capabilities and subject-matter experts, such as electricians, doctors, forgers, engineers, chemical engineers, biologists, interpreters, and computer experts.[68] Each of these skills provides the underground with increased capabilities as required:

- Electricians can help develop sophisticated explosive firing devices and wiring complex explosive devices
- Doctors and veterinarians that can establish clandestine hospitals for wounded insurgent members
- Forgers to make fake documents
- Civil and mechanical engineers to help determine target vulnerabilities, such as bridges, buildings, and factories
- Chemical engineers to help fabricate explosives; biological engineers that can develop biological weapons
- Local interpreters hired by the counterinsurgents that can gain access to valuable intelligence that can be passed to the underground through clandestine communications methods
- Computer experts that can establish clandestine communications mechanisms on the Internet or to hack hostile security forces websites

Lastly, the auxiliary member's daily lives may provide the underground with capabilities that would otherwise not be at their disposal, such as:

- Large trucks for moving quantities of logistical supplies hidden within legally carried cargo
- Newspaper printing presses that can be used after hours to produce clandestine propaganda
- Hospital and veterinary clinics that can be used for after hours surgery of critically wounded insurgents
- Shop and restaurant owners that can provide security and intelligence support by locating their shops to over watch critical military targets or routes used by the counterinsurgents
- Shipping and fishing vessels that allow coastal movements of the insurgent members

This list names only a few examples; there are endless possibilities. The auxiliary provides the bulk of the movement's operational, logistics, and intelligence support and specialized capabilities. While support to the underground is less resource intensive for the underground, support to the guerrillas—the third component—requires significant resources depending on the size of the guerrilla force.

The guerrillas are the overt arm of the insurgency.[69] The size and organizational structure of guerrilla elements are dependent on their environment—rural guerrillas are generally more hierarchical in structure, along normal military lines. In rural insurgencies, the guerillas may operate as small guerrilla bands or as near-conventional guerrilla armies made up of thousands. The difference in size depends on the security environment, the physical environment, and the ability to successfully and openly organize large guerrilla formations without fear of interdiction.[70] The guerrillas may even have modern heavy weapons, such as tanks and artillery, further clos-

Figure 2. Palestinian Alnasser Salah aldeen Brigades army for Popular Resistance Committees attend training organized by the Hamas movement in Gaza City. Photo used by permission of Newscom.

ing the gap between the security forces and the guerrilla forces. In Iraq and Afghanistan, the insurgents have operated largely as small guerrilla bands, only massing for extremely short periods of time to ensure they do not become decisively engaged, while attempting to overwhelm local security forces. This is in contrast to the Northern Alliance that on 9/11 had extremely large formations and capabilities, to include tanks and artillery that made them a near peer to the Taliban, and thus had resulted in years of static defensive lines. In urban areas, guerrillas may be referred to as "urban guerrillas," but differ from the direct action cells described in the section on the underground above because the guerrillas have less lethal-skills training, as well as less tradecraft training. Although not as well trained as the underground direct action cells, the urban guerrillas hide amongst the "urban jungle," operating in small cells, and largely utilizing low-signature hit-and-run tactics, to include the employment of improvised explosive devices, small arms, sniper systems, and man-portable, short-range anti-tank weapons. However, urban insurgencies, or combined rural and urban insurgencies, where the rural environment is not conducive to concealing or supporting large overt guerrilla units, such as the desert environment of Iraq, are inherently more clandestine than overt.[71] In both cases, the clandestine elements of the insurgency resort to clandestine cellular networks as their organizational framework for operational security in the high threat environments. Despite their form being more clandestine and cellular than the rural guerrillas, urban guerrillas differ from the direct action cells found in the underground due to their lack of specific training or clandestine methods. The difference lies in the ease of replacing "urban guerrillas" versus replacing specialized direct action cell members. The urban guerrilla cell members have limited training and are generally easy to replace. They are likely hired to conduct attacks on the counterinsurgent forces that do not require significant training, but are extremely high risk. Their vulnerability and ability to be replaced have earned them the nom de guerre "low-hanging fruit."[72]

Thus, the three components of an insurgency are critical to the understanding and operation of clandestine cellular networks. Although the overt guerrillas capture most of the attention of the counterinsurgents, it is the clandestine cellular network, composed of the underground and auxiliary, which are the critical elements for a successful insurgency. Guerrillas can ultimately be easily replaced over time. Underground and auxiliary members cannot be as easily replaced. The clandestine cellular nature of these networks minimizes their signature in order to reduce the chance of being detected and interdicted by the counterinsurgent, while the cellular nature ensures that counternetwork operations do not threaten the rest of the organization. The following sections will focus on the cellular nature or form of the networks.

The Development and Growth of Clandestine Cellular Networks

To understand the form of clandestine cellular networks it is important to understand how they develop and grow. The ARSOF model of Mao Zedong's Protracted War Theory explains how an insurgency develops and matures. The ARSOF model consists of the latent and incipient phase, guerrilla warfare phase, and war-of-movement phase.[73] During the latent and incipient phase, the core organizes into clandestine cellular networks around a common goal based on an ideology and/or grievance, to establish the underground. The underground develops an auxiliary, and starts conducting non-violent subversion, such as demonstrations, walk-outs, and strikes, and types of non-lethal sabotage of key infrastructure or factories causing production slowdowns.[74] This non-violent action then transitions to violent political action in the form of terrorism, intimidation, and coercion.[75] As the movement begins to develop and the security situation is at a level that overt elements can operate with some freedom of action, then the movement develops guerrilla units as its overt fighting force.

This transition into the guerrilla warfare phase, where overt attacks increase with the introduction of more conventionally organized guerrillas, marks the point where the underground is sufficiently large and robust enough to not only support an overt element, but recover if the overt element suffers losses. Even though the insurgency has moved into the guerrilla warfare phase, the underground continues to operate and grow in order to gain resources, grow into new target areas, and build shadow government elements. In some cases, the establishment of shadow government elements takes place under the noses of the counterinsurgents, if there is poor population control, or the underground can wait until areas are liberated by its own guerrilla force, and then establish the shadow government.

If guerrilla units are able to grow to large sizes, and become near-peer competitors to the state security forces, then the insurgency transitions into the war-of-movement phase. In this phase, the counterinsurgent is unable to effectively counter the insurgency, the insurgency is now capable of conducting decisive military operations, and the insurgency begins to prepare for transition into power. At this point, there is less need for compartmentalization or signature reduction one would find in a clandestine cellular network in the latent-incipient and guerrilla warfare phases.[76] At this overt end of the organizational scale, the units are operating with maximum efficiency and low security because they can sustain more losses than in the earlier phases. Efficiency here is compared to the other end of the insurgent organization scale, where the clandestine cellular networks reside within the underground. At the clandestine

> *If guerrilla units are able to grow to large sizes, and become near-peer competitors to the state security forces, then the insurgency transitions into the war-of-movement phase.*

end of the scale, as Valdis Krebs notes, "covert networks trade efficiency for secrecy."[77] Regardless of the success of the overt elements, a portion of the clandestine cellular network will remain to provide a viable base from which to re-grow the movement should there be a catastrophic defeat of the overt movement during the war of movement phase. Those elements deemed critical to supporting the war of movement will move to overt support to increase efficiencies, while other portions critical to survival will remain hidden and inefficient for good reason—ensured survival of the movement. If unsuccessful during this phase, the movement will be pushed back to a preceding phase, and the underground will once again be required to increase compartmentalization of the underground and auxiliary to support the guerrillas, or if decisively defeated, return to the latent-incipient phase.

Although this model is an outstanding one for the overall movement, or what John McCuen calls "strategic phases," Department of the Army Pamphlet (DA PAM) 550-104 provides a five-phased model that provides sub-phases for the underground elements.[78] The first three phases of the 550-104 model take place in the latent and incipient phase of the protracted war phasing. In phase one, "the clandestine organization phase," the core organizes the clandestine cellular networks.[79] Phase two, the "subversion and psychological offensive," includes non-violent subversion, such as spreading rumors, strikes, boycotts, demonstrations, and limited terrorism.[80] Phase three, the "expansion phase," begins the transition from clandestine cellular networks to the development of guerrilla units, with phase four, the "militarization phase," marking the introduction of overt guerrilla forces.[81] The fifth phase of underground growth, and really the steady state for the underground until success or failure is "the consolidation phase," in which the underground movement creates shadow governments, including meeting humanitarian, legal, security, religious, and education needs, as well as collecting taxes, or other resources and manpower from the population.[82] The underground uses its shadow government to establish control of areas, and as its name implies, it could be in parallel with current government programs. The intent in this final phase is to gain and maintain control of the human terrain—the population. The underground will continue to spread its control, almost a reverse application of the popular oil-spot counterinsurgency strategy, to starve the government of support.[83]

Elements of Insurgent Clandestine Cellular Networks

The underground, as its name implies, begins with the core leadership and cadres that develop the ideology, find a common grievance to garner popular support, and develop a strategy and organizational pattern based on the physical, human, and security environments. The organizational structure of the underground is based on the clandestine cellular network model, with different networks and cells assigned functions. Examples of the different types of underground networks are shown in Figure 3:

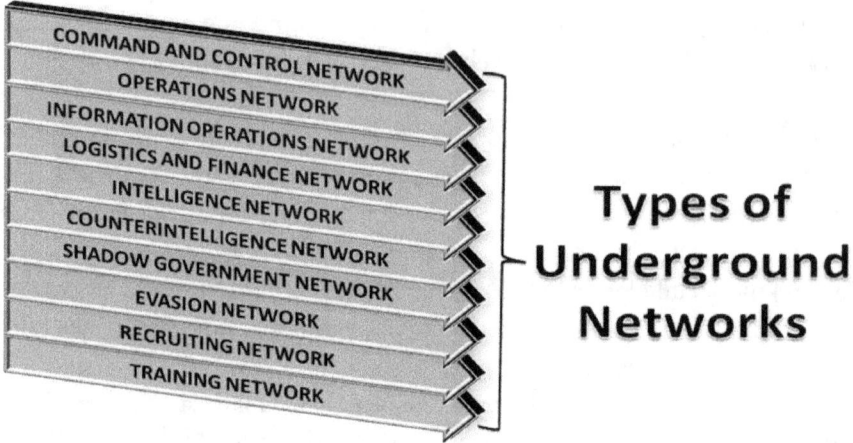

Figure 3. Types of Underground Networks[84]

The core networks primarily operate within urban areas, with networks that extend to rural areas providing support in conjunction with the auxiliary. Underground elements operate almost entirely clandestinely, with a few exceptions being the overt political wings. Although there may be no visible link between the overt and clandestine elements from the perspective of the outside observer, there are likely strong ties, with the true leaders being hidden within the clandestine network providing guidance and direction to the representatives in the political wings.

The clandestine cellular network is based on the core building block, the cell. The cell size can differ significantly from one to any number of members, as well as the type of interaction within the cell, depending on the cell's function. There are generally three functions—operations, intelligence, and support.[85] The cell members may not know each other, such as in an intelligence cell, with the cell leader being the only connection between the other members (see Figure 4).[86] In more active operational cells, such as a direct-action cell, all the members are connected, know each other, perhaps are friends or are related, and conduct military-style operations that require large amounts of communications (see Figure 4).[87] Two or more cells linked to a common leader are referred to as branches or sub-networks of a larger network, as shown in Figure 4. Cells linked to a common leader are also referred to as "cells-in-parallel" or "cells-in-series" (see Figure 5).[89] For example, operational cells may be supported by an intelligence cell or

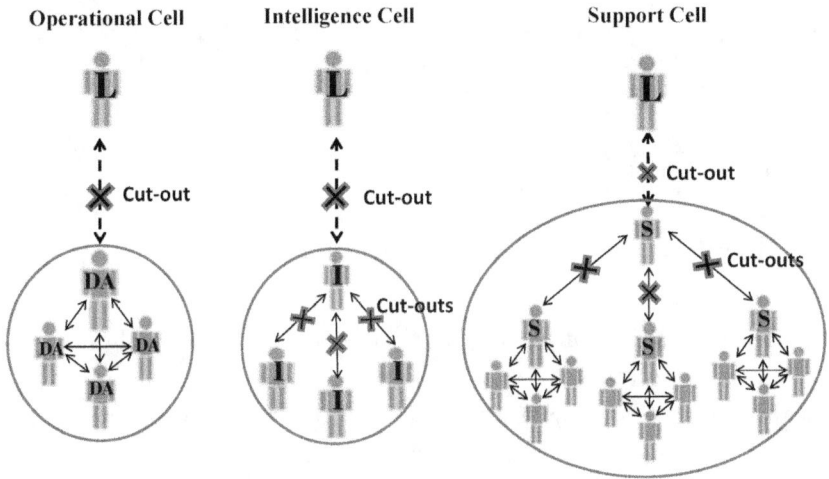

Figure 4. Examples of Functional Cells: Operational, Intelligence, Support[88]

logistics cell as shown in Figure 5. In some cases, as in Figure 4, the alternate cell-in-parallel could have the same operational function as the primary cell and is available to the branch leader if the primary cell is interdicted.[90] If the cells within the branch are compartmented from each other, but have a role or function that builds on the other, they are referred to as "cells-in-series," with the branch leader coordinating their actions (see Figure 5). Cells-in-series are primarily for manufacturing, safe-house networks, evasion networks, or weapons procurement and emplacement.[92]

Building upon the branch is the network, which is made up of multiple compartmentalized branches as shown in Figure 6, generally following a pattern of intelligence (and counterintelligence) branches, operational

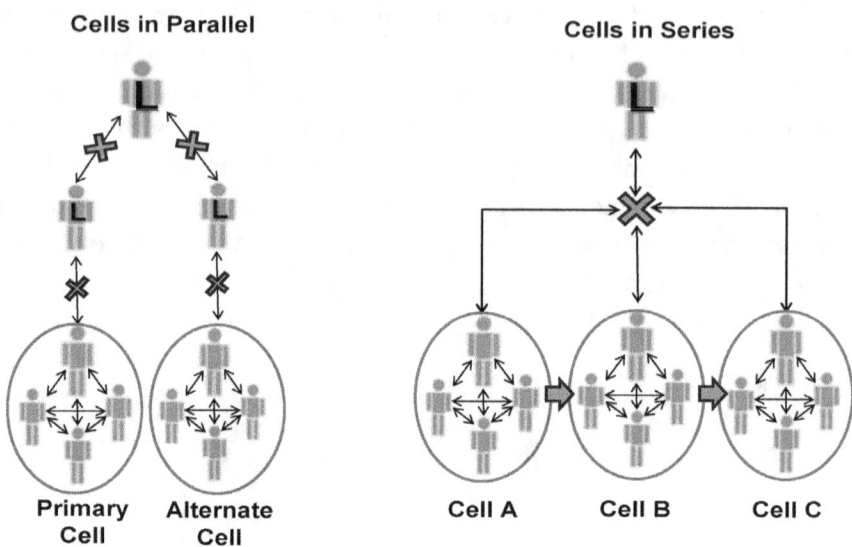

Figure 5. Examples of Cells-in-Parallel and Cells-in-Series[91]

branches (direct action or urban guerrilla cells), support branches (logistics and other operational enablers like propaganda support), and overt political branches or shadow governments.[93] Complex branches or networks, such as the example network in Figure 6, have a combination of cells and branches, and even individuals—especially leaders, in series and in parallel. The network has a leader that coordinates the efforts of his clandestine intelligence, logistical support, and operational cells, as well other elements, such as a local political wing or guerrilla force. He also has his own force-protection support, such as safe-house keepers, that operate the different locations he uses to hide during his daily routines. The leader may switch between his safe houses daily or every few hours to minimize the threat from counterinsurgents pinpointing his location.[94] The leader may also have an evasion network that no one else in the organization knows about that he can use in an emergency. If he is the leader of a sub-network, also known as a branch, from a larger network, then he coordinates his efforts with his superior, who is responsible for a number of similar branches or sub-networks. This pattern continues to the core of the movement as shown in Figure 6. These networks generally radiate out from the core members of the movement. They do not grow randomly or uncontrolled, nor do they follow strict mathematical growth—defined as self-organization—all of which can be found in different types of information-age networks.[95] Instead, they grow purposefully, either to link into supportive populations, to move into an area that the insurgents want to gain control of as part of their strategy, or to gather intelligence around a specific target. As they grow, the leadership of the network decentralizes tactical decisions but maintains operational and strategic control.

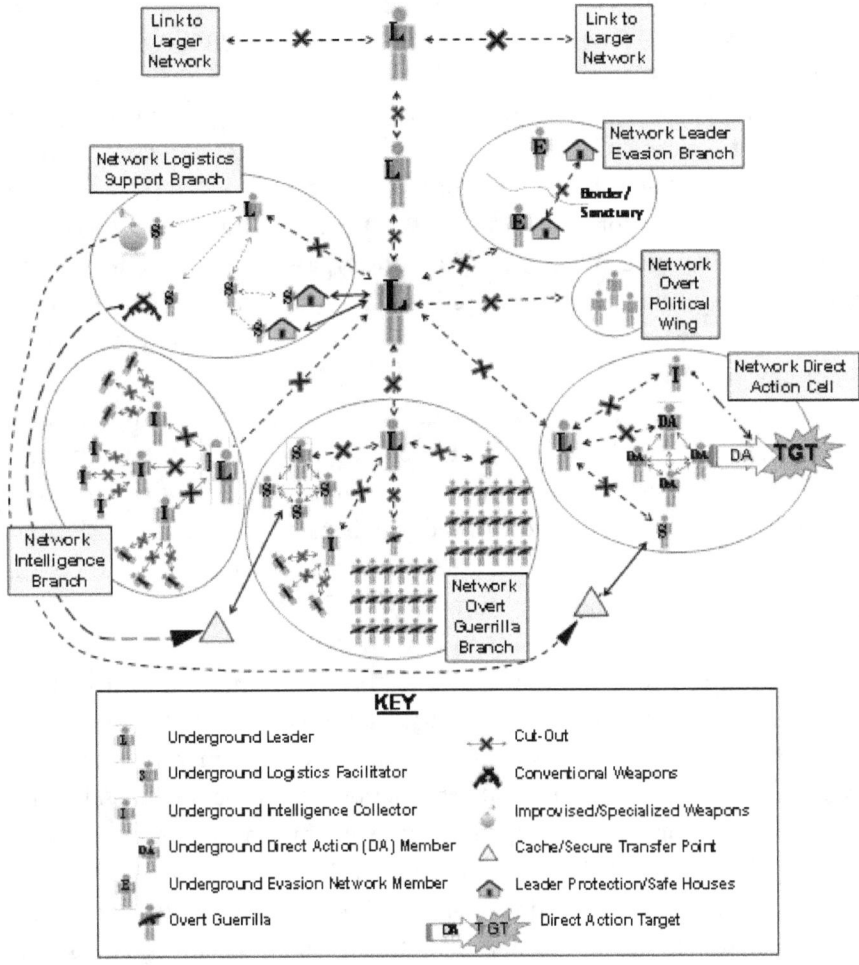

Figure 6. Example of an Insurgent Network[96]

Clandestine cellular networks are largely decentralized for execution at the tactical level, but maintain a traditional hierarchical form above the tactical level.[97] There is an ongoing debate as to whether clandestine cellular networks are "networks" as understood today, or hierarchies.[98] Some experts believe they are flat organizations with near-real time interaction across the entire organization, others believe they are "leaderless" as well, with all members being relatively equal.[99] This monograph proposes that insurgencies are inherently hierarchies, but decentralized hierarchies. The core leadership may be an individual, with numerous deputies, to preclude decapitation strikes, or the core leadership could be in the form of a centralized group of core individuals, which may act as a centralized committee made up of core members. The core could also be a type of coordinating committee of like-minded insurgent leaders who coordinate their efforts, actions, and effects for an overall goal, while still maintaining their own agendas.[100] Without centralized control, the organization would not be able to effectively develop a strategy based on ends, ways, and means, since each individual or group would not be bound to the common vision, which a hierarchy provides.[101]

Decentralization at the tactical level is due to the difficulty of real-time command and control within a large clandestine cellular network. As a result of compartmentalization and low signature for survival, network leaders give maximum latitude for tactical decision-making by cell leaders to maintain tactical agility and freedom of action based on local conditions.[102] This theory is not dissimilar from U.S. military doctrine, and the idea of mission type orders with commander's intent to give subordinates the maximum leeway for conducting tactical actions, and advocates for subordinates to take initiative. The network leaders accept the risk that the subordinates may make mistakes, but due to compartmentalization, the mistake will largely remain local. The elements that make a mistake may pay for their error, by being killed or captured, but the rest of the network will remain secure. The key consideration of the underground leader, with regards to risk versus maintaining influence is to expose only the periphery tactical elements to direct contact with the counterinsurgents. This allows local adaptability to counterinsurgent tactics, as well as agility to maintain pressure on the counterinsurgents without getting decisively engaged or exposing the clandestine network. In addition, the network leadership can replace the members of the tactical cells relatively easily if they are killed or captured. It is much harder to replace core members, but a good network leader will ensure redundancy in critical capabilities, such as leaders, to make sure the movement remains viable even if key leaders are killed or captured.

Structural Compartmentalization in Clandestine Cellular networks

The key concept for organizational form is compartmentalization of the clandestine cellular network.[103] Compartmentalization means each element is isolated or separated from the others.[104] Compartmentalization separates not only the clandestine elements from each other, but more importantly perhaps, the clandestine elements from the overt elements.[105] The ultimate goal for the organization is that no counterinsurgency operation can threaten the overall survival of the organization. There is always a portion of the clandestine network remaining upon which to re-grow the movement if necessary. It is the focus on long-term survival, or the "winning by not losing," which truly defines why this organizational form is used. As Trinquier noted, "The security of a clandestine organization is assured by rigorous compartmentation [sic]."[106]

Structural compartmentalization is in two forms. First, is the *cut-out*, which is a method ensuring that the counterinsurgent is unable to directly link two individuals together.[107] Second, is through lack of knowledge—no personal information is known about other cell members, so capture of one does not put the others at risk. For example, aliases may be used and/or organizational or operational information is only provided to members on a need-to-know basis.[108] The 1966 DA PAM 550-104 refers to this second method as the "fail-safe principle."[109] The amount of compartmentalization, as mentioned above, depends largely on the threat environment in which the organization operates, including physical terrain, the human terrain—made up of active and passive supporters, neutral observers, and those deemed hostile to the movement—and the perceived threat from operations of the counterinsurgency force. As shown in Figure 5, compartmentalization also separates the overt elements, the guerrillas, and the political wings of the insurgency from the clandestine elements as a further fail-safe.

The key for compartmentalization is that if any person in the network is detained, they have little, or preferably no, direct knowledge of the other members of their cell or network.[110] The soundness of the networks is directly dependent on the network leaders, their experience and training in establishing and maintaining the compartmentalization, and the training they have provided to their subordinates. As Figure 5 depicts, the sound clandestine networks with strong compartmentalization have a much better chance of survival even if the counterinsurgent is able to detect and interdict a cell or individual. Against the strong network the counterinsurgent quickly runs into the cut-outs and is unable to identify additional targets. In the weak clandestine network, the exact opposite is true; the members are easy to detect and due to lack of compartmentalization, they are quickly interdicted by the counterinsurgent force suffering from numerous breakdowns in compartmentalization.

In any cell where the members must interact directly, such as in an operational or support cell, the entire cell may be detained, but if the structural compartmentalization is sound, then the counterinsurgents will not be able to exploit the cell to target other cells, the leaders of the branch, the sub-network, or overall network (see Figure 7 and Figure 8).[111] Thus, the structural compartmentalization protects the rest of the network. If however, the network has poor structural compartmentalization, then the counterinsurgents will be able to interdict a greater number of individual network members, until the counterinsurgents run into a portion of the network that is sufficiently compartmentalized to stop further exploitation (see Figure 7 and Figure 8). Poor compartmentalization, characterized by direct communication with members of other cells in the same branch or members of other networks, results in a complete failure of the purpose of compartmentalization as depicted by the dashed lines between the cells in Figure 7 and Figure 8.[113] This results in a catastrophic "cascading failure" and the disruption, neutralization, or destruction of multiple cells, branches, or even the entire network may ensue (see Figure 7 and Figure 8).[114]

In addition to the structural weakness in compartmentalization between supposed clandestine elements, there is inherent weakness in structural compartmentalization between overt and clandestine elements of the movement. In this case, leader interactions or interactions between the underground, auxiliary, and guerrillas increase the chance of detection since the overt elements won't be as comfortable interacting with the underground and auxiliary elements in a clandestine fashion, greatly increasing the risk. There are also weaknesses when different networks from different insurgent groups work together (see Figure 7; the dashed line provides an example).

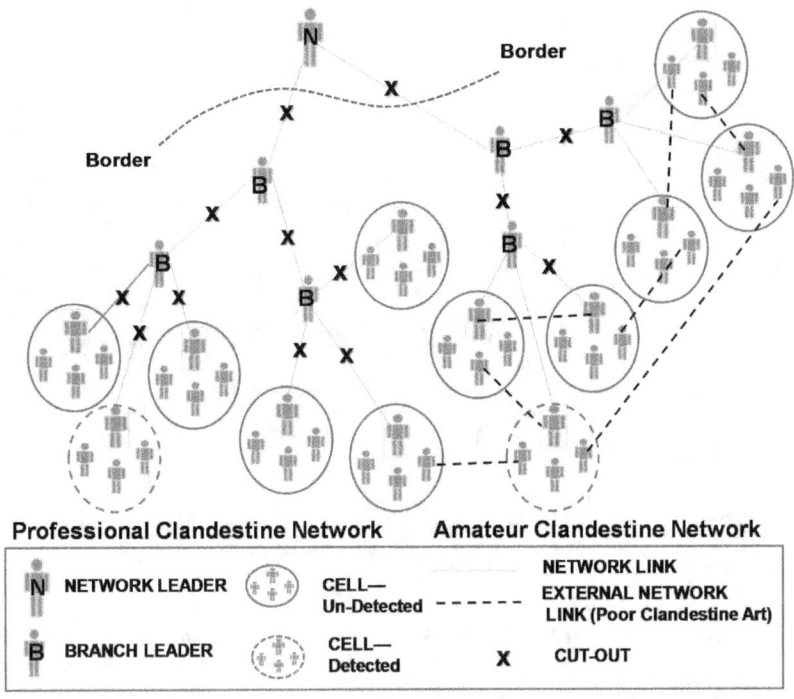

Figure 7. Examples of Compartmentalization prior to Counternetwork Operations[112]

In the case of different insurgent groups working together, there is always an increased risk, since the compartmentalization in one group may not be as good in another, allowing a counterinsurgent operation to exploit this weakness if discovered and thus penetrate one network through another.

There may also be issues with compartmentalization when external support networks, either nation-state or non-state actors, provide combat, direct, or indirect support to the insurgent network, which is considered UW.[117] If the two networks can build a solid relationship and the external support network is clandestinely sound, then the weakness is limited (depicted in Figures 7-9). If not, then the weakness of the network also puts the external support at risk as shown in Figure 8. The primary concern is with direct network-to-network interaction between a representative of the external supporter and one from the indigenous insurgency. For the nation state providing one of the types of external support—indirect, direct, or combat support—the representative could be an intelligence officer or

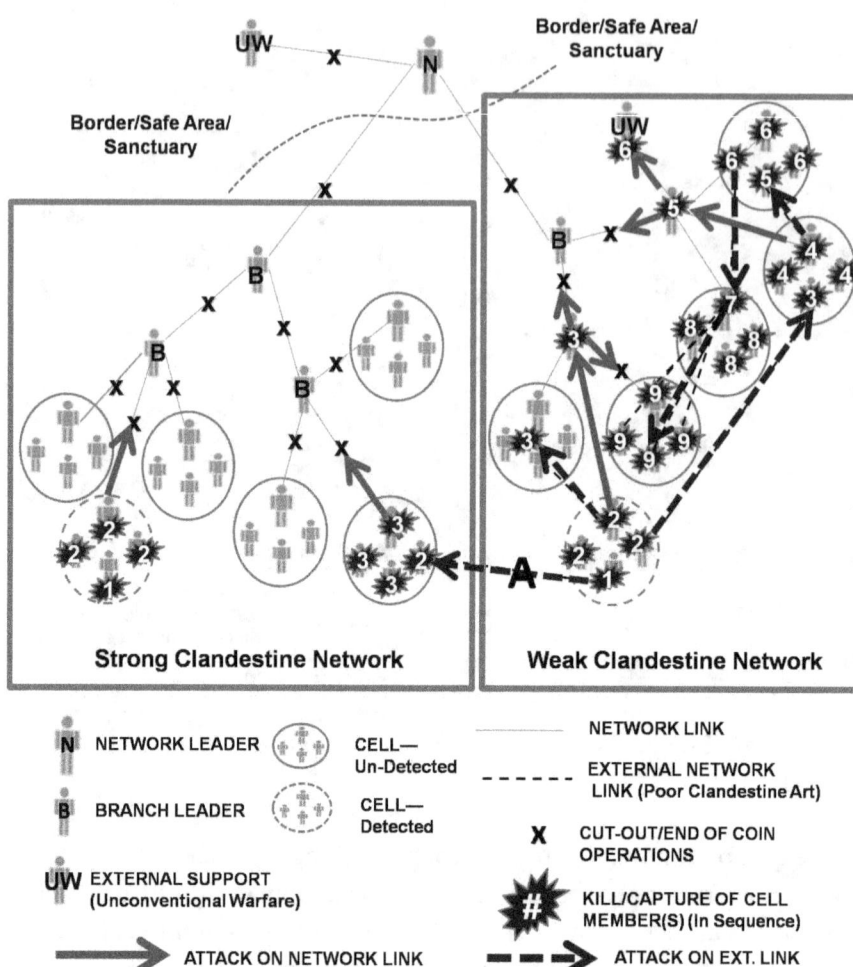

Figure 8. Examples of Compartmentalization during Counternetwork Operations[115]

members of a military special operations unit, interacting with their contacts in the insurgency within the country of conflict, in a sanctuary area, or in a third-party country, depending on a threat. This type of network interaction is not new. There are contemporary examples from Iraq, where Iranian nefarious activities have included the direct linkage from the insurgency to the Iranian Ministry of Intelligence and Security and Iranian Republican Guard Corps special operations forces.[118]

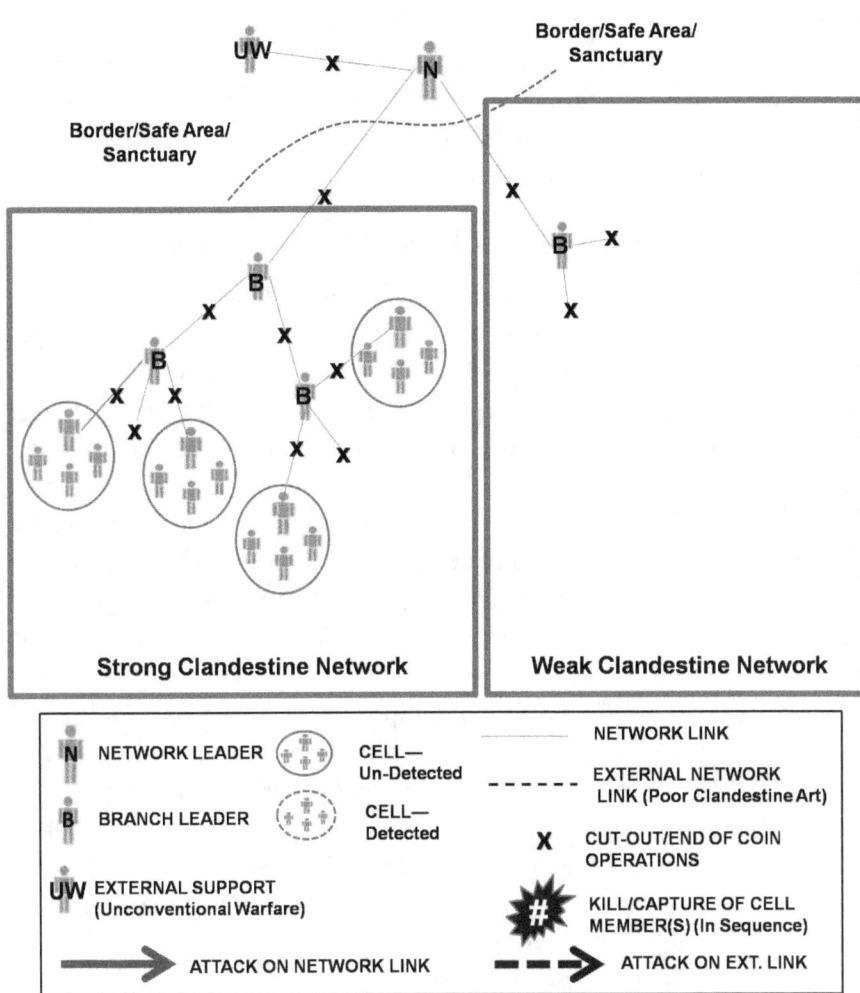

Figure 9. Examples of Compartmentalization post Counternetwork Operations[116]

Since 9/11, external support to insurgency has also fundamentally changed with the addition of a global non-state actor, al-Qaeda, and its unconventional warfare efforts to support like-minded inter-state insurgent groups within the context of a larger global insurgency strategy. This type of support is best symbolized by Abu Musab Zarqawi's network in Iraq. Similar al-Qaeda efforts can be found in other countries, such as Afghanistan, Pakistan, Indonesia, Algeria, Somalia, and the Philippines. In both state and non-state external support to insurgency, unconventional warfare is being conducted by the supporting state or non-state against the government fighting the insurgency.[119] Proper compartmentalization will largely protect all the organizations involved if employed correctly, or at least will forestall catastrophic cascading failures across the link between the external support network and the insurgency.

Understanding the Scale of Clandestine Cellular Networks

Compartmentalization is obviously critically important and a fundamental of clandestine cellular networks. The next step in understanding these types of networks is to understand the "scale," or size of these networks. While the U.S. doctrine focuses on the guerrilla forces, which can reach large sizes, it fails to appreciate the scale of the underground required to support these overt forces and the complex task of ensuring compartmentalization for what can be extremely large clandestine organizations. Based on the Special Operations Research Office study in 1963, the size of undergrounds in historical examples of insurgencies have been surprisingly large: Palestine (1948)—30,000; Philippines (1946)—100,000; Greece (1946)—675,000; Malaya (1950)—90,000; Algeria (1956)—21,000; Yugoslavia (1940)—50,000; and France (1946)—300,000.[120] Contemporary examples provide similar numbers—in the first four years of the counterinsurgency efforts in Iraq, from 2003-2007, an estimated 80,000 insurgents were killed or captured.[121] Although this number is not subdivided into guerrillas, auxiliary, and underground, it shows the magnitude of the insurgency, and based on the previous ratios, it could be interpreted that a large percentage of this number are underground and auxiliary members.

To understand how these underground elements get so large, the classic children's fable *The King's Chessboard* provides a practical model.[122] In this fable, the king offers to pay a wise man for his services, but the wise man, initially refusing payment, is forced to accept some type of compensation. The wise man asks to be paid in rice for each square on a chessboard, starting at one grain, and doubling at each square.[123] The king readily accepts the offer, failing to understand the exponential growth that will take place as the grains of rice begin to double, much in the same way there is a general failure to understand the exponential growth of clandestine insurgent networks. The amount of rice begins to grow from one grain of rice, to two, then four, then eight, then sixteen, and so on, until the number becomes so large it costs the king all of his rice.[124]

The same thing happens within clandestine cellular networks, but is rarely understood. Each leader develops subordinate leaders who then become branch leaders as they develop their own subordinate leaders, and with this, the scale or potential size begins to emerge. Thus, the first piece of rice represents the initial core leader that at the second square develops two subordinate leaders, who on the third square, each develop two subordinate leaders, and so on. Each square represents new subordinate leaders and the last square represents subordinate leaders plus their cells. In just five squares, there would be 16 cell leaders and their respective cells at the edge of the organization: 15 branch leaders or sub-network leaders, and the original network leader. Imagining this metaphor applied in the context and scope of the historical examples of insurgency above, or against contemporary examples such as Iraq and Afghanistan, and the scale of the clandestine cellular networks begin to emerge.[125]

Figure 10. Shebab fighters participate in a military exercise in northern Mogadishu's Suqaholaha neighborhood 1 January 2010. Photo used by permission of Newscom.

Open and Closed Clandestine Networks

Once scale is understood, it is imperative to understand one final concept related to clandestine cellular network organization—open and closed networks and cells.[126] Networks, sub-networks, and cells, can be described as open or closed. Understanding if a network or cell is open or closed helps the counterinsurgent to determine the scale, vulnerability, and purpose behind the network or cell. An open network is one that is growing purposefully, recruiting members to gain strength, access to targeted areas or support populations, or to replace losses. Given proper compartmentalization, open networks provide an extra security buffer for the core movement leaders by adding layers to the organization between the core and the periphery cells. Since the periphery cells on the outer edge of the network have higher signatures than the core, they draw the counterinsurgent force's attention and are more readily interdicted by the counterinsurgent, protecting the core. Open networks also increase the "reach" and "mass" of the clandestine network by allowing purposeful growth into areas that may be untenable by overt elements of the insurgency and the ability to increase the insurgent threat faced by the counterinsurgents.

Closed cells or networks on the other hand have limited or no growth, having been hand selected or directed to limit growth in order to minimize signature, chances of compromise, and to focus on a specific mission. While open networks are focused on purposeful growth, the opposite is true of the closed networks that are purposefully compartmentalized to a certain size based on their operational purpose. This is especially pertinent for use as so-called "terrorist cells," made up of generally closed, non-growing networks of specially selected or close-knit individuals. Closed networks have a set membership that generally does not change, and is indicative of cells, or special-purpose networks, such as the members of the network involved in 9/11. Closed networks have an advantage in operational security since the membership is fixed, and consists of trusted individuals. The compartmentalization of a closed network protects the network from infiltration by the counterinsurgents. In the case of a specific mission, the closed network or cell operates like an insurgent or terrorist group special operations-like entity. Despite the precautions taken to protect the closed cell or network, its fundamental drawback is that once the cell has been penetrated or infiltrated by the counterinsurgent, then the entire closed network or cell is exposed to interdiction.

Since 9/11, much of the discussion on clandestine adversaries focuses on so-called "terrorist cells," failing to differentiate between open and closed networks, such as al-Qaeda as a global insurgency—an open network, and the al-Qaeda members that made up the 9/11 hijackers—a closed network—popularly described as a "terrorist cell or network." Noted theorist Valdis Krebs mapped the 9/11 network, including the 19 hijackers and numerous individuals who provided logistics support for the operation, yet never understood that this was a closed network.[127] Krebs's study has been used by numerous theorists to develop attack methodologies for use against so-called terrorist networks and insurgent networks, failing to realize the closed networks and open networks have different forms, function, and logic, and thus require different applications of counternetwork theories.[128] Interdiction of a closed network versus open network is much different, with the closed network being the easiest to disrupt and defeat because the membership is fixed and can be attritted. This is not possible with an open network that still has access to resources, either internally or externally.

Both examples highlight the fundamental difference between open and closed clandestine cellular networks, respectively. To understand the relative scale, it is also imperative to identify whether a network is open or closed.

Using a Metaphor to Understanding Clandestine Networks

Using a tree as a metaphor for all elements of an insurgency provides a model to visualize and develop a deeper understanding of the concepts presented thus far. Using Figure 11 as the model, an insurgent underground grows much like a new tree. It is an open network, purposefully growing. Before the tree sprouts, it must have a large enough root system to support the weight of the tree as it grows. The root system must continue to grow to ensure that it not only supports the trunk, branches, and canopy, but that it is big enough, broad enough, and with enough surface area to ensure maximum nutrients within the soil can consumed to support the tree's growth. In this case, the main roots represent the underground, while the additional root growth and support to the tree is very much like the role of the auxiliary. In this metaphor, the thicknesses of the different parts of the tree are directly related to the effectiveness of organization compartmentalization and resiliency from attack.

During this initial growth, just as with a tree, the insurgency is at its most vulnerable point, which would equate to the latent and incipient phase of an insurgency. As the tree continues to grow the main root begins to grow purposefully to ensure it has tapped into all available resources for the "tree" or "movement" in the case of the insurgency. With growth, the relative thickness of the trunk, roots, and branches continue to increase corresponding to the strength of the insurgent components they represent. The trunk above ground represents those parts of the insurgency as it grows from a clandestine movement with the first above ground elements being at the greatest risk, including the thin trunk, branches, and the initial leaves. As the tree grows and gets stronger and bigger the overtness increases, indicative of the increasing thickness of the tree trunk. The ultimate war of movement phase example of a tree is the oak tree with its trunk that can be measured in feet and a root system that extends well beyond the radius of the canopy.

As the tree continues to increase in size, leaves begin to grow, much like the cells and guerrilla units at the outer edge of the organization. Similar to an insurgency, the leaves are closed systems on the tree, but the tree, and the movement alike, can grow numerous cells and guerrilla units. These can be knocked off, blown off, or cut off with minimal effect on the tree. The lost leaves, like cells and guerrilla units, are replaced as required. The leaves have purpose as edge elements, direct contact with the sun, just as the insurgent cells and units to have direct contact to their intended target.

The final component of the metaphor is the fruit of the tree which equates to the closed cells previously described. These closed cells or networks are made up of hand-selected individuals with a specific mission. As with fruit, this closed system is delicate, and any penetration of the "skin" and exposure to the inside of the "fruit" will be devastating. Once it has fallen away from the tree to complete its purpose, it is its own self-contained entity that either completes its mission or, if the skin of the fruit is breached prior to the purpose being carried out, will rot, and the seeds will die. For a global insurgency like AQ, the fruit representing the closed cell can be used for kinetic operations, like the 9/11 strikes, or the fruit can represent the cadre of individuals that "fall from the tree" to develop additional movements, in AQ's case through the application of unconventional warfare to support insurgencies or resistance organizations fighting apostate governments in and around the desired caliphate.

If the tree metaphor is used to describe an interstate insurgency only, then outside support, or unconventional warfare, by nation states or non-state actors, can be described in the metaphor as fertilizer, tree stakes, insecticide, or even efforts to dissuade loggers from cutting the tree down. Each of these is not natural to the tree or its surroundings, but each is aimed at helping the tree, and in this example the insurgency, in some way. The fertilizer can represent logistics and financial support that allows the underground to grow and better support the overt elements. The tree stakes represent the external advisors who come in to help organize, train, and support the insurgency. The tree sticks can either help guide the insurgency to be more effective, or literally pull the insurgency back into line with the external supporter's national interests. The bug spray represents the UW effort to counter threats to the organization directly. Last is the dissuasion of the logger, who could represent a third party country that is providing support to the government fighting the insurgency. In this case, the country conducting UW would leverage all elements of its national power to keep the third party nation disrupted or coerced so that it is unable or unwilling to bring its combat power, in this case a chain saw, to operate against the insurgency in support of the host nation.

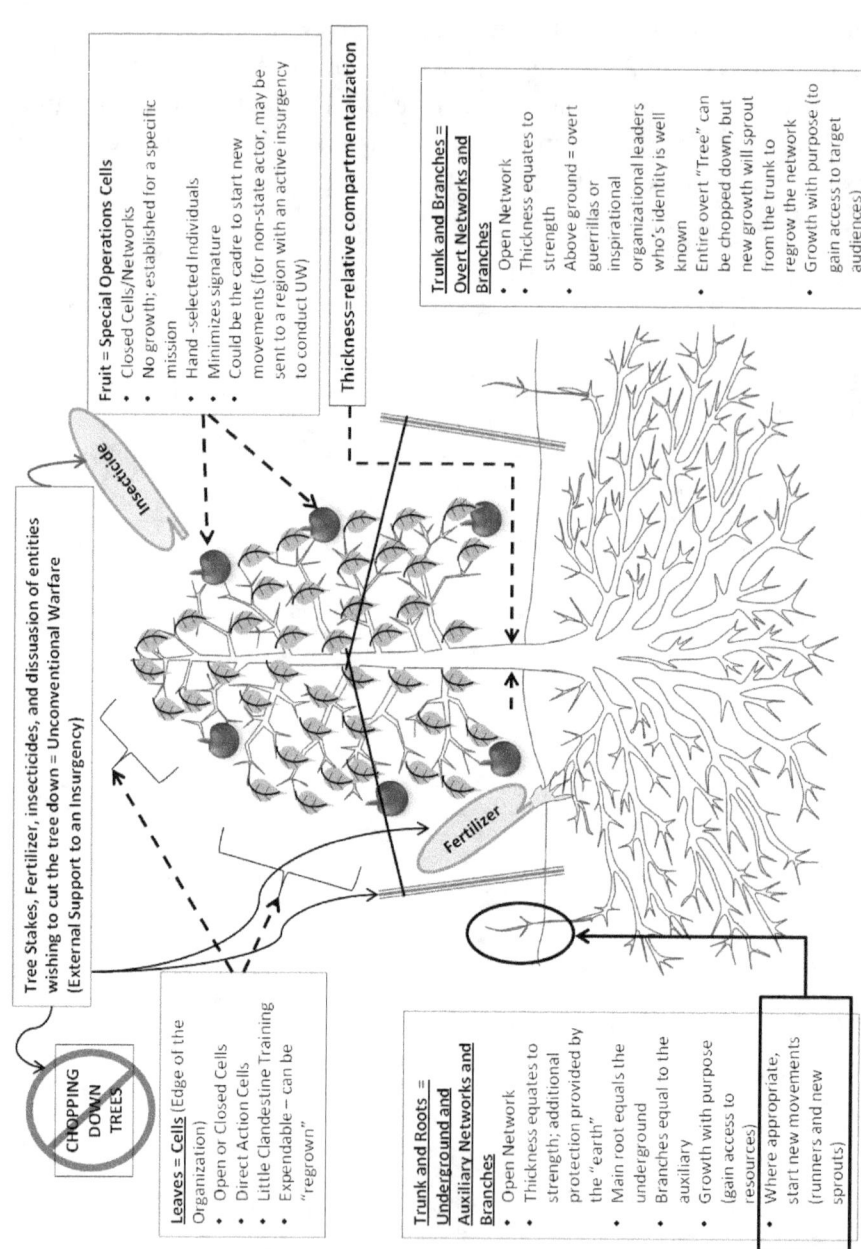

Fruit = Special Operations Cells
- Closed Cells/Networks
- No growth; established for a specific mission
- Hand -selected Individuals
- Minimizes signature
- Could be the cadre to start new movements (for non-state actor, may be sent to a region with an active insurgency to conduct UW)

Thickness=relative compartmentalization

Trunk and Branches = Overt Networks and Branches
- Open Network
- Thickness equates to strength
- Above ground = overt guerrillas or inspirational organizational leaders who's identity is well known
- Entire overt "Tree" can be chopped down, but new growth will sprout from the trunk to regrow the network
- Growth with purpose (to gain access to target audiences)

Tree Stakes, Fertilizer, insecticides, and dissuasion of entities wishing to cut the tree down = Unconventional Warfare (External Support to an Insurgency)

Insecticide

Fertilizer

CHOPPING DOWN TREES

Leaves = Cells (Edge of the Organization)
- Open or Closed Cells
- Direct Action Cells
- Little Clandestine Training
- Expendable – can be "regrown"

Trunk and Roots = Underground and Auxiliary Networks and Branches
- Open Network
- Thickness equates to strength; additional protection provided by the "earth"
- Main root equals the underground
- Branches equal to the auxiliary
- Growth with purpose (gain access to resources)
- Where appropriate, start new movements (runners and new sprouts)

Figure 11. Insurgent Movement Tree Metaphor (Author's figure)

Section Summary

As this section highlighted, clandestine elements of an insurgency use form—organization and structure—for compartmentalization. The compartmentalization, from which the term cellular comes from, relies on isolating individuals and information to ensure minimal impact on the organization if individuals are detained or killed. Thus the cellular structure protects the network from counternetwork operations to ensure the long-term viability of the organization. It is this factor alone that challenges the current counternetwork operational trend of targeting high-value individuals. These operations are well within the tolerance of clandestine cellular networks.

In order to fully understand the form of clandestine cellular networks, this section also explained in detail the different elements of the insurgency, as well as the phasing, scale, and opened and closed networks of the clandestine network of an insurgency. Using the three-phase model of insurgency, the development and growth of the insurgent movement from the latent and incipient phase to the guerrilla warfare phase, and ultimately the war of movement were explained. Where doctrine fails to understand the importance of the underground and auxiliary, this monograph provided examples of the size that these two elements have historically reached, and how open clandestine networks grow with purpose. It also explained the aspects of closed networks, and how network theorists have incorrectly used closed systems to develop counternetwork theories that are being applied to open networks.

Lastly, this section provides a metaphor for describing the different structural aspects of an insurgency, specifically related to the clandestine cellular networks. The intent of this metaphor is to provide the reader a model upon which to gain further insights into the structural elements of an insurgency. With this metaphor, a general model is established to explain the organizational compartmentalization and the different elements of the insurgency. This allows a more detailed understanding of the non-structural elements that make up the functional compartmentalization of clandestine cellular networks discussed in the next section.

3. Function of Clandestine Cellular Networks

As explained above, clandestine elements of an insurgency use form—organization and structure—to compartmentalize and minimize damage due to interdiction by counterinsurgents by limiting information distribution and interface with other members of the organization. Clandestine networks use function—clandestine art or tradecraft—to minimize signature and thus detection by counterinsurgent forces, and facilitate the communication between compartmented elements. In essence, *functional* compartmentalization, in addition to compartmentalization through organizational *form*, as explained above, are the ways that insurgents protect themselves to ensure long-term survival—the "logic" behind the use of the organizational form and function—in order to defeat the government or occupying forces.

Function is defined as "an action or use for which something is suited or designed."[129] It is the function of clandestine art or tradecraft to keep the network signature low so the daily interactions of the network members remain undetectable by the counterinsurgent force.[130] These functions in clandestine cellular networks revolve around minimizing signature and detection of the interaction of members of the network and their operational acts. The ability of insurgents to do this effectively has noticeable effects. For example, in 2005, RAND Corporation's Bruce Hoffman published an analysis of the insurgency in Iraq, concluding that the insurgency was a cluster of uncoordinated and disconnected local insurgent groups with no centralized leadership.[131] As he explains, "The problem in Iraq is that there appears to be no such static wiring diagram or organizational structure to identify, unravel, and systematically dismantle."[132] However, in hindsight it is obvious that the assumption of a disconnected insurgency was incorrect. Instead, the insurgency was primarily made up of clandestine cellular networks, applying excellent tradecraft to remain hidden and to hide the connections between the individuals in the movement. Thus the unseen linkages or networks that connected the seemingly distributed cells were the clandestine infrastructure (form), further protected by clandestine arts (function), to minimize signature so that the clandestine cellular networks were not readily visible to the counterinsurgents as shown in Figure 12.[133]

The visible parts of the networks were only the cells that were in direct contact with the counterinsurgent forces, at the periphery or edge of the organization, which practiced poor tradecraft and were detected and inter-dicted (see Figures 6-8). Units that conducted operations against these cells had success until they hit a compartmentalization mechanism, or cut-out, that stopped the exploitation, thus marking the boundary or edge of the clandestine organization (see Figure 7 and Figure 8).[134] Interestingly, where one cell or network is effectively interdicted, in a short period of time, a new cell or network appears to take its place.[135] As one former battalion commander commented to the author in 2006, "My battalion would [kill or capture] a cell and a new one will take its place within a couple of weeks at the most."[136] In hindsight, it is obvious that the insurgency was connected and coordinated behind the veil of the clandestine space.[137]

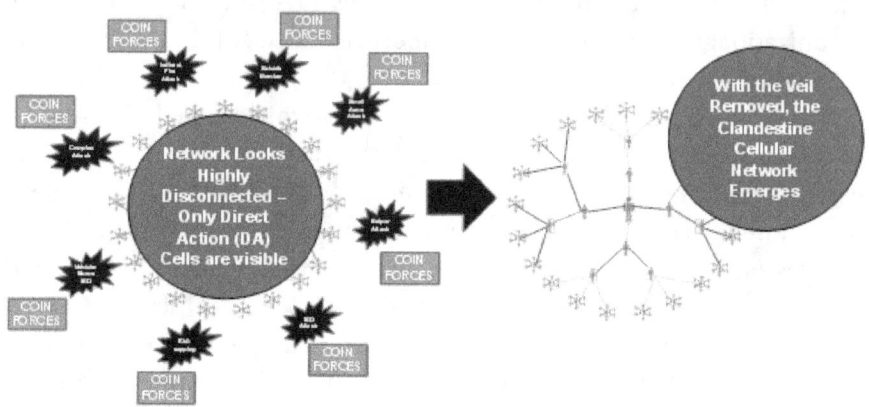

Figure 12. The Emergence of the Clandestine Cellular Network[138]

Although much of this hidden network relied on structural form to protect the network from pursuit by the counterinsurgents, the function of clan-destine arts or tradecraft kept the signature so low that even experts like Hoffman did not realize the magnitude of the insurgency and its internal coordination.

Therefore, just as important as understanding clandestine cellular net-works' organizational compartmentalization, it is imperative to understand the functional compartmentalization as well. To facilitate the functional compartmentalization, clandestine techniques or tradecraft are used for the following: to conduct indirect or impersonal communications in order to *functionally* compartmentalize the organization; to minimize the signature of person-to-person communications, or "personal communications;" to conduct counter-surveillance; to reconnect the network when key leaders are detained or killed; to clandestinely recruit new members in order to purposefully grow the organization or replace losses; to hide key individuals using safe houses; to provide security for locations, such as meeting places and safe-houses; and lastly, to facilitate clandestine skill training between the superior and subordinates.[139]

Impersonal Communications

Impersonal communications, also known as cut-outs, functionally compartmentalize the networks as an additional precaution to the organizational forms of compartmentalization explained in the previous chapter.[140] Impersonal communications, as the name implies, is anything other than face-to-face contact between two members of the organization.[141] Impersonal communication is a method of ensuring that two individuals never come in direct contact, and thus cannot be physically linked to one another.[142] Impersonal contact includes passive and active methods, the difference being in the type of signature produced.[143] Passive methods include mail or dead-drops, live drops, and clandestine codes or signals hidden within different types of media.[144] Active methods include short or long-range radios, phone, and Internet, all which emit signals that can be more readily detected by technologically capable counterinsurgents.[145]

Passive measures are used to minimize signature in high-threat environments. Couriers are the most secure means of transmitting messages or moving items, such as weapons, between two individuals.[146] The key requirement for couriers are their ability to move some distance, including through counterinsurgent population-control measures, such as checkpoints, without arousing suspicion.[147] Women and children may be used as couriers to decrease suspicion and the chance of search if moving sensitive items or written information.[148] Although couriers are one of the most secure methods, they and their messages can be intercepted, as was the case with the letter sent from al-Qaeda's Ayman al-Zawahiri to Abu Musab Zarqawi in Iraq that exposed a rift between the al-Qaeda core leadership and Zarqawi over Zarqawi's tactics against the Shi'a in Iraq.[149]

The second method of impersonal communication is the mail drop, also known as a letter drop or dead drop.[150] In this method, one member of the network places a message or item at a certain location, the drop site, which for larger items could be a cache. The deliverer then alerts the receiver, through other clandestine means, to pick up the item, resulting in no personal contact between individuals.[151] French counterinsurgency practitioner Roger Trinquier provides a description of the Algerian underground use of mail drops: "Carefully kept apart from other elements of the organization, the network was broken down into a number of quite distinct and compartmented branches, in communication only with the network chief through a system of letter boxes."[152] Although mail or letter drop describes the idea of leaving a letter or package in the Western mindset, and at times may include literally using the post office, this wording also symbolized that some unconventional locations may act as "mail boxes." Orlov provides some examples of the use of unconventional hiding places:

> Hiding places, such as a hollow in a tree…or a deep crack in a wall… or a hole bored in a public monument, take the place of mailing addresses….A special system of 'indicators' is used to orient each agent as to the specific hiding place where a message is awaiting him….The 'indicator' consists of a number or a symbol written on a wall, a park bench, or somewhere inside a railway station, post office, or public telephone booth.[153]

Thus the "item" is dropped off by one individual and then hours or days later, when the other individual sees the "indicator," he can recover the item, place an "indicator" signaling that he has retrieved the item, and thus ensures that both parties know the status of the communication while maintaining the anonymity.[154]

The third method of passive communication is the so-called "live drop."[155] The difference between a dead drop and live drop is that there is a person at the drop site that secures the item being passed between members.[156] This person is the cut-out, passing the item to the other member when they come to the location after being alerted that the item has been left with the live drop through some indicator or signal. As Prikhodko explains,

> When communicating by means of a live drop there is no personal contact….Operational materials from [deliverer]…are passed through a special person who more frequently than not is the proprietor of a small private business (book shops, antique dealers, [drug stores], etc.). The [receiver] visits the live drop…only after a

special signal. The proprietor of the live drop places the signal after receiving the items.[157]

The danger of this method is that if the individual that is the live drop is discovered, he has a direct link to the other member and may provide information that can lead to the interdiction of the other member, but only if he has enough information on the other members, such as names, addresses, or acquaintances. If not, then the "live drop" method works as an effective cut-out.

Clandestine codes are the fourth method and can be used across different types of media to alert other cell members or pass information passively.[158] In print media, this could include ads or announcements in newspapers in which the information in the ad is a code that the other cell members understand.[159] In World War II, the Allies extensively used the nightly British Broadcast Corporation overseas radio broadcasts to the resistance forces in Europe to pass information clandestinely on resupply drops and operational directives. These included the messages that only had meaning for the intended receiver, based on a code word intermingled in the broadcast, such as a forewarning of an impending parachute resupply drop to the resistance on a certain drop zone.[160] This same theory causes intelligence agencies to conduct in-depth analysis of broadcasts by al-Qaeda core leadership to see if there are any hidden messages.[161] Finally, code words can be innocuously inserted into emails or telephone conversations that for example could provide warning of security forces approaching or execution orders to conduct operations against pre-approved targets.[162] Regardless of the means, it is the passage of information while maintaining a low signature that makes these very difficult to counter.

Active methods of impersonal communications—short- and long-range radio, Internet, landline, and cell phone—provide a much faster means of communications that has to be weighed against the increased risk of detection and interdiction by technologically-sophisticated counterinsurgents.[163] Short- and long-range radio transmissions have largely been replaced by phone. However, radios may be the only method of rapid communication in areas where there is no phone coverage. Radios may also be necessary if the instant passage of messages is required, such as an early warning alert of counterinsurgency forces moving into the area. Telephones, both landline and cell, have a role in impersonal communication, with the disadvantage of producing a signal which a security force could monitor. Phones can also be combined with passive measures, such as code words.[164] The Internet has opened a new clandestine playing field, but like other active measures, there are still dangers due to an electronic signal. Thus, instead of being a revolutionary adaptation, like the information age network theorists posit, the Internet provides the ability to disseminate information and ideology quickly and is another tool for communicating, but it comes with associated risks. The same clandestine techniques presented here have also been adapted to the cyberspace, including using cyber dead drops.[165] However, like other active measures, there are dangers due to the electronic signatures that can be detected by the counterinsurgents.[166] For example, Jihadists have attempted to clandestinely hide their webpage by piggybacking on other non-nefarious websites, often without the webmaster's knowledge, but they have been discovered in some cases.[167] Despite the strengths of active methods, such as rapid communications and long-distance reach, they significantly increase the danger for the insurgent due to the signals emitted that may be detectable by a technologically-advanced adversary.[168]

Personal Communications

Meetings between members of a cell or network, who would normally be separated by one of the methods of compartmentalization, greatly increase the vulnerability of the two members.[169] However, despite the risks, there may be times when a clandestine leader needs to meet in person with his subordinates, instead of using an impersonal means, to gain better situational awareness, train the subordinate, assess the subordinate, or when the clandestine recruiting process explained below requires personal communications with potential recruits.[170] As I. E. Prikhodko explains from the perspective of an intelligence officer working with his subordinate agent,

> Only by personal contact can the case officer study the agent better, analyse [sic] his motives, check on and control his activities, and finally—and this is of great importance—instruct the agent, train him in new methods and in professional [clandestine] skills, develop him, and exert an influence on him through personal example.[171]

Due to the vulnerability, meetings must be thoroughly planned including: identifying a meeting location, planning the routes of both individuals to and from the meeting location, establishing security to counter surveillance during the individuals' movements to the location, as well as having security around the location to give early warning and a plan if the meeting fails to take place.[172] As Swiss insurgency expert H. von Dach Bern notes, "meetings of [underground] members must be prepared at least as carefully as a raid, for they constitute a 'special type' of operation."[173]

Counter Surveillance

Surveillance is the observation of a person or place to gain or confirm intelligence information, conducted by foot, vehicle, aerial, cyber, mechanical, and from a fixed location.[174] This section will describe the counter surveillance techniques practiced by the insurgent to defeat the counterinsurgent's attempts at surveillance.[175] Counter surveillance methods are those taken by the individual members for three purposes: to keep from being surveilled while conducting insurgent-related activities; to determine if under surveillance; and to thwart active and passive surveillance in order not to expose other members, operations, or physical infrastructure of the network, such as safe houses or caches.[176] During the Cold War, surveillance was a mix of stationary, foot, and vehicle surveillance.[177] These types of surveillance techniques can be used against cells and networks operating outside zones of conflicts where the threat to the surveillance team is minimal. However, due to the difficulty of counterinsurgent elements safely conducting foot or vehicle surveillance in a high-threat counterinsurgency environment, today's insurgents have to contend more with aerial surveillance, both manned and unmanned, as well as other types of intelligence-collection platforms. During the hunt for Abu Musab Zarqawi in Iraq, for example, an aerial-surveillance platform followed Zarqawi's spiritual advisor as he conducted a counter surveillance operation in which he quickly switched vehicles.[178] However, the aerial-surveillance package watched this counter surveillance maneuver and followed the spiritual advisor to where he met with Zarqawi, a fatal application of counter surveillance technique, leading to both of their deaths. Regardless of the types of surveillance employed by the counterinsurgents, low- or high-technology, the same basic counter surveillance principles apply.

The best method of counter surveillance is to keep from being detected in the first place. As DA PAM 550-104 noted in 1966,

A former underground leader has suggested that while it is difficult to completely escape modern surveillance methods, there are many ways to mislead the surveillants. The underground member, wishing to minimize risks and chance factors, attempts to be as inconspicuous as possible and refrains from activities which might bring attention or notoriety. He strives to make his activities conform with the normal behavior and everyday activities of the society in which he lives.[179]

Having cover stories that provide a good reason for being in an area is one of the best methods of countering surveillance. For example, a clandestine network could use a delivery company driver as a courier, or could move large items, such as weapons, hiding them within the shipment, delivering the information and items as the driver makes his daily or weekly rounds within an urban area.[180] Along the same lines, a larger shipping company may ship items to numerous locations within a country or even across borders, giving the clandestine network long-range operational reach to support larger networks spread out over geographic regions or even into sanctuary areas in neighboring countries. The possibilities are endless.[181]

Soviet clandestine operations expert I.E. Prikhodko refers to these measures as "counter-surveillance check routes which afford the most favourable [sic] opportunities for the detection of surveillance."[182] As Prikhodko explains, these check routes provide the clandestine operator a method of determining if they are under surveillance through a combination of traveling by different means (car, bus, train) and through different areas (urban, rural, congested, and sparsely populated) that would expose any surveillance package by forcing them to betray their activity.[183] If no surveillance is detected after a certain period of time using the check route, the clandestine operator can be reasonably sure that he is not being followed.[184] This technique is used by both the leader and his subordinates if they are to meet, or conduct any other type of activity that may compromise other members or infrastructure if surveilled. This technique could also be used to move to and from safe sites, caches, or dead drop locations. If surveillance is detected, then the clandestine operator cancels the meeting or other planned activities so as not to expose the other elements of the network or he attempts to lose the surveillance and continue the operation.[185]

Emergency Methods for Re-connecting the Network

Cellular or compartmentalized networks are by their nature resilient to attacks that kill or capture single individuals, to include key leaders, facilitators, or specially-skilled individuals, who have superiors and subordinates. These individuals will be referred to as nodes for clarity in this section. By compartmentalizing the organization, the damage done by counterinsurgent operations is minimized and allows for the re-connection of the network above and below the lost node. In this case, when a node is removed, emergency clandestine communications measures must have been pre-arranged by the leader prior to his death or capture, to ensure that his subordinate and superior can link up.[186] This prearranged method is developed in such a fashion that the instructions do not lead to the compromise of either party.[187] Thus, the reconnection procedure must be systematic and clandestine principles applied throughout. Without some type of secure and clandestine mechanism to reconnect the network, the network can be successfully fractured, and would be indicative of poor clandestine practice.[188] In some cases, a network can reconnect if the members know each other well, but again, this ability is indicative of an insecure network that is operating more on luck than on any type of set clandestine procedures.[189]

In a well-structured clandestine cellular network, emergency communication methods are established throughout the organization from the higher level to the lower levels, as the organization grows, minimizing the threat of fracture.[190] The reconnection process can take place in four ways:

- Top down—the lost node's superior to subordinate
- Bottom-up—subordinate to superior
- Through a third party or intermediary, using a process similar to a live drop, providing a method for anyone in the organization to regain contact with the core network
- Through common knowledge of the other network members outside the individual's normal cellular chain of command, which happens in networks that are made up of individuals that know each other well[191]

Regardless of the method, the superior and subordinates may not know each other, and thus have to rely on pre-arranged recognition signals, codes, and specific actions when they meet.[192]

The first method is used when the higher level leader, the superior of the killed or captured node, makes contact with the subordinate through a pre-arranged method, such as a phone call and code word, or a visible signal, much like the one described by Orlov for marking a dead drop.[193] The superior establishes the special marking in a pre-designated location after the node has been removed. The subordinate knows that when he sees this emergency signal, he is to carry out the previously agreed upon action given to him by his former leader—such as calling a certain number and using a code name—going to a certain location at a specific time to meet some-one.[194] Once the two elements have linked up, the superior can provide the subordinate with further instructions on what to do and how to maintain contact. The superior may elect to promote the subordinate to replace the lost node, replace the lost node with someone else, or fill the role himself. Regardless of the method, a superior practicing good clandestine technique will immediately establish a new form of cut-out to protect the superior and subordinate once the meeting is complete.[195]

In the second method, the subordinate contacts the superior.[196] This method would be most likely used if the leader of the subordinate was captured, and the subordinate was worried that his leader may provide information leading to the subordinate's arrest. This may force the subordinate to flee the operational area, nullifying any attempt by the superior to use pre-arranged signals in the old area of operation. In this case, another set of pre-arranged emergency procedures would be used, where the subordinate established an emergency signal at a pre-designated location to alert the superior. As before, this would lead to the link up of the two elements, and the reconnection.

The third method, much like the live-drop described above, would be a location, such as a business, provided to all the members of a network, to go in case of lost contact.[197] A code word or code name would then be used to alert the owner or workers of the need for the individual to get in touch with a network leader.[198] Once the subordinate initiates the code word, he is given further instructions on how the superior would contact them to affect the link up. This method is risky for the location owner and workers since it acts as a funnel for multiple individuals to use to get in contact with network leaders. The individuals working at the location could be detained in an attempt to get them to provide information on the superior's location. This was the main method of the Allied evasion networks during World War II, where pilots were given a location to go to in order to get funneled into the network, but the Axis was able to infiltrate numerous agents acting as Allied pilots to fully expose these networks.[199] If the superior has established a solid cutout between the location and himself, then he, theoretically, is protected. The superior can further protect himself by controlling the location of the meeting site and by establishing inner and outer security to observe if the subordinate is under surveillance prior to committing to the meeting.

In many cases, the superior and the subordinates do not know each other, which requires further application of clandestine methods during the actual physical link-up to ensure positive identification. It is the physical act of contact with an unknown subordinate that puts the superior at greatest risk.[200] He has to assume that the subordinate may have been detained, turned by the counterinsurgents, or perhaps provided them with the re-contact plan, and they have inserted an infiltrator, taking advantage of the lack of direct knowledge of the individual.[201] Due to this threat, the link-up is one of the most dangerous acts, and thus requires further application of clandestine methods.[202] It would be easy to meet at a pre-designated isolated location; however, this would make counterinsurgent surveillance easier if the subordinate was in fact working for them. Instead, the superior wants to blend in and use the human terrain to his advantage.

To do this he will establish a meeting location, likely in a very public place, such as a restaurant or market, with numerous escape routes.[203] The location would also provide an environment in which his inner and outer security elements could also blend into, or maybe even be part of the chosen environment, such as storeowners, sellers, and buyers in the market, or other jobs that are natural for the surroundings, in order to identify counterinsurgent surveillance. If the superior has indirect contact with the subordinate and can pass messages, he may provide detailed instructions, describing the exact route to take and providing a set of signals for recognition, emergency abort, and safe signals, as well as an alternate meeting plan if there is a reason the meeting cannot be carried out.[204] These instructions may also be passed through dead or live drops as well. If conducted correctly, the inner and outer security should be able to identify surveillance or determine if the subordinate is "clean." If they discover surveillance is following the subordinate, then the meeting is cancelled, and the superior escapes.[205] If not, then the superior and subordinate meet after exchanging recognition signals and code words to verify identities, and then they can begin the process of reestablishing the network.

The final method happens in poorly compartmentalized networks and in networks built on pre-existing friendships, acquaintances, or groups, such as clans and tribes. In these cases, it is possible for individuals to re-link into the network through known individuals. This technique, with numerous links that bypass any cut-outs, such as members of one cell that interact with other cells, is indicative of a network with poor compartmentalization and clandestine practices, and could generally be categorized as an unsecure network that is operating at a very high risk. Sherri Greene Ottis' *Heroes: Downed Airmen and the French Underground* describes this method being used by some evasion line networks in WWII to return downed pilots to allied control.[206] In some cases it worked, mostly out of luck, but for the most part, it led to the destruction of multiple escape lines in World War II throughout occupied Europe.

It should also be noted that regardless of the method of reconnection, once the link-up is successful, the superior will determine how best to reestablish the intermediate node. This will be done either through promoting the subordinate of the lost node, bringing in an outside individual that had not been previously part of the network, or simply by the superior taking over the role himself.[207] The course of action is likely determined prior to the meeting so that the superior only has to expose himself once during this emergency reconnection. If he can reestablish the cut-out simultaneously, then once the two depart, the network is generally safe again. If either individual is picked up leaving the site, they will not know the whereabouts of the other one. With the cut-out reestablished and the new reconnection instructions and clandestine communications instructions passed to the subordinate, the network can once again reconnect if one of the individuals is captured or killed by security forces soon after the face-to-face meeting.[208]

Clandestine Recruiting

Although there is a perception that clandestine networks are largely made up of trusted and known friends and family members, reality throws this logic into a spin.[209] For an insurgency to be successful, it must increase in size and control.[210] While family and friends provide an added sense of security through loyalty bonds, and may well make up the members of the core group, few insurgent movements can be successful only having the support of their close friends or family, including tribes and clans. They must branch out and increase their popular support in order to affect large political change. To do this, the organization must grow with purpose in order to gain access to the population for resources, to replace losses, and to gain access to areas to target counterinsurgent forces. Thus, unlike information-age networks that grow randomly or without any control mechanism, such as the Internet or social networks, clandestine networks grow with purpose—identifying low-risk individuals that bring skills, resources, intelligence, or access to targeted areas.[211] These individuals go through a process of clandestine recruiting.[212] Unlike the strong links between trusted individuals that have developed trust relationships prior to partaking in nefarious activities, clandestine recruiting is largely a method for recruiting unknown individuals or acquaintances of others, a form of social networking, and thus a weak link to the clandestine recruiter.[213] Generally, the recruiter is a network member that is purposefully gaining more links. The recruiter may or may not be a network leader, recruiting his subordinates directly. He could be a member of the core network who has the right kind of background or natural talent for recruiting, who recruits new members based on organizational needs, and then passes the recruit off to a network leader for actual operational control.[214] This may in fact protect the network if the recruiting effort goes bad and a potential recruit turns in the recruiter. In this case, having good cut-outs between the network and the recruiter further protects the network.

The key for the clandestine recruiter is to never let on that he is recruiting for the insurgency until he has used his skills to identify, assess, and possibly test the candidate for recruitment. He must be reasonably certain that the recruit will accept his recruitment offer when finally approached.[215] The recruiter is looking for a recruit who has a personality for clandestine work; the right motivation, trustworthiness, and loyalty; special skills or military background; access to a specific target location, population, intelligence, or resource of importance to the insurgency; and has the proper background—ideological, ethnic, or religious—to support the core movement's agenda.

> The key for the clandestine recruiter is to never let on that he is recruiting for the insurgency until he has used his skills to identify, assess, and possibly test the candidate for recruitment.

In some cases, if there is doubt about the recruit's willingness to work with the insurgency, the recruiter may have embarrassing background information to blackmail the recruit or he may simply gain compliance through coercion and threats to kill the recruit or members of the recruit's family if he does not cooperate.[216] If the person declines the offer to work with the insurgents, then the same methods of blackmail or coercion can be used to keep them from going to the counterinsurgents.

Another purposeful growth model, other than recruiting, includes insurgent leaders marrying into families, tribes, or clans, to gain instant rapport, loyalty, commitment, and access to the resources of the group, much like the monarchies of old, where the sons and daughters would be married to link kingdoms or countries.[217] This technique depends on the cultural and societal norms, but may effectively unite groups quickly. This is a favorite technique of al-Qaeda to try to quickly gain the trust and backing of tribes, as was evident in al-Anbar in the year leading up to the "Anbar Awakening."[218]

Safe Houses

Safe houses are used as part of core members' daily pattern of hiding from counterinsurgent forces, or if members are under pressure of pursuit by counterinsurgents and "need to go underground."[219] Safe houses are locations that should not draw attention, nor be readily connected to any pattern of insurgency or criminal activities.[220] These locations give the user a place to hide or stay that has a built-in but invisible inner and outer security ring to provide early warning and protection.[221] Key leaders may use a series of safe houses daily to allow them to change location regularly to thwart attempts by counterinsurgency forces to interdict them. They generally move based on either early warning or within the amount of time they believe it would take for the counterinsurgents to gather intelligence, develop a plan, get approval, and conduct the operation. This may cause them to move every few hours or days, depending on the perceived threats, the capability of their early warning, and how good an escape plan they have. It is not uncommon to hear of insurgent leaders who move every few hours each day to make sure that they are not captured.[222] If the counterinsurgents conduct operations against the safe house, but miss the insurgent leader, then the insurgent leader knows that he cannot reuse that safe house location without an increase in risk since the house may be under surveillance, or the informant that provided the information that drove the counterinsurgents to raid the location may still be active.

As shown in Figure 6, safe houses are maintained by a subordinate leader as part of an operational support network.[223] The person that maintains the safe house is not involved in any other organizational functions so as not to draw attention and jeopardize the safe house.[224] The leader uses the safe house or safe location as randomly as possible so as not to provide the counterinsurgent with a distinguishable pattern amongst several safe houses.[225] At each location, a system of emergency signals would alert the user whether the location is safe or not. For example, safe signals may be the "predesignated [sic] placement of shutters; flower pots; arrangement of curtains; open or closed windows; or clothes hanging on clothes lines."[226] Changes to these pre-designated signals would alert the leader that the site was not safe. The leader may also establish a personal evasion network or line, also depicted in Figure 2, in which he establishes all the safe houses, safe-house keepers, and movement plans himself so no one else in his organization knows.[227] This gives the network leader the ability to escape if the rest of his organization is detained. The evasion may be interstate, or extend over borders into sanctuary areas or other international locations.[228]

Security at a Location

Security at any location, such as meeting sites, safe houses, and dead drops, provides a means of early warning to give the network members an opportunity to escape or not approach the location.[229] To conduct this type of operation, the member responsible for establishing the location must have good communications with the members conducting security in order to get near real-time warning of impending danger. Two security rings are established—inner and outer.[230] Inner security is responsible with immediate security around the site, and may be armed to disrupt any counterinsurgent operations that penetrate the outer security without being detected in order to give the underground members time to escape. Outer security observes likely routes into the location that the counterinsurgents may use. A system for communicating must be established, and may include cell or telephones, short-range radio, signals, or runners.[231] There should also be an agreement on actions of the security elements and the individuals at the location, whether to fight, flee, or if the security elements will fight the counterinsurgents to give the key network members a chance to escape.[232]

In some cases, the security elements may simply be passive, watching key counterinsurgency locations such as bases or airfields, or the security elements may be individuals infiltrated onto one of these installations—such as cooks, maintenance personnel, laundry facility workers, contractors, or even interpreters— that provide a form of outer-ring early warning, but within the enemy camp.[233] This passive security measure could include overhearing conversations between soldiers about upcoming missions or information found in the trash. In the case of locally hired interpreters, they may even be directly briefed on upcoming missions against the network that they actually work for, thus providing the ultimate security and situational awareness for the network leaders. If the interpreter deems the threat to be immediate, then he can risk calling the network leader direct with the warning. In the case of infiltrators whose duty does not allow for daily movements on and off the counterinsurgent installation, such as the interpreter who may have ongoing operations or strange hours due to ongoing operations, or the information is not time sensitive, then another clandestine communication method can be used. For example, other local-hires purposefully infiltrated onto the installation by the network leaders with regular daily schedules may be the courier between the network leaders and interpreter or other intelligence gatherers. In this case, they may use a dead or live-drop procedure to pass the information, or the courier may use the same method to pass instructions from the leaders to the agent.

Other passive outer-ring security techniques may include recruiting business owners whose businesses sit astride likely counterinsurgent routes, or even outside the gates of counterinsurgent installations. The movie *Blackhawk Down* also provides an example of outer security, where a young boy is paid to sit and watch over the airfield. He then phones the cell leader to report activity, in the case of the movie, the over flight of a large helicopter assault force departing the airfield.[234] Passive security can consist of anyone who does not draw the counterinsurgents' attention.

Clandestine Skills Training

New and old members must be continually trained and tested on the clandestine methods above to make sure they are not violating the clandestine procedures of the network.[235] As Prikhodko explains,

> Clandestinity in agent operations is directly dependent on the indoctrination...keeping in mind the main objective: to offer assistance, to show how to fulfil [sic] his assigned task better and more securely, [and] to help correct mistakes he has committed or eliminate inherent shortcomings.[236]

However, the best training is risky due to the fact that the leader and subordinate must meet in person until the leader is confident that his subordinate is trained.[237] This training can take place in any secure location and may include any of the functional skills described above, as well as operational skills required by the individual, such as the employment of new weapons systems.[238] As Prikhodko notes, "The [network, branch, or cell leader's] task is to train [subordinates] properly and to transfer [them] to impersonal forms of communications in good time."[239]

If the insurgency is receiving external support and is directly working with intelligence or special operations personnel from the external supporter, personnel may undergo specialized training in tradecraft and other clandestine operational capabilities. During the Cold War, communist insurgent leaders received extensive training by communist regimes, especially the Soviets, such as the courses taught at the Lenin School.[240] The ability of nation-states and non-state actors to provide this type of in-depth training continues today, but much more covertly, to provide plausible deniability, such as the training provided by Iran to Iraqi Shi'a insurgents.[241] This training may be conducted simply during a personal meeting between the underground member and the external support representative locally or could include training outside the country of conflict, such as in sanctuaries or other locations chosen by the external supporter. Person-to-person training, as noted above, increases the risk of all parties involved, but training at external sites provides the opportunity for intense training to be conducted while not under pressure from the counterinsurgents.

The last method is training conducted almost as independent study, including reading historic literature, manuals produced by the insurgent organization, or online references. Obviously, this is the least preferred method for training individuals in the organization. The Internet provides a balance, with the ability to provide video, and rapidly disseminate new tactics, techniques, and procedures, but still far from perfect. Without controlled or precision distribution to desired individuals, the counterinsurgent can view and learn from these as well. The medium for distribution may also not reach isolated individuals. Stratfor's Fred Burton correctly identifies the problems with this type of training in tradecraft,

> While some basic [clandestine] skills and concepts…can be learned in a classroom or over the Internet, taking that information and applying it to a real-world situation, particularly in a hostile environment, can be exceedingly difficult. The application often requires subtle and complex skills that are difficult to master simply by reading about them: The behaviors of polished tradecraft are not intuitive and in fact frequently run counter to human nature. That is why intelligence and security professionals require in-depth training and many hours of practical experience in the field.[242]

Thus, freedom of movement is paramount for clandestine leaders to gain access to their network members, especially new members, and provide clandestine training if they expect their subordinates to survive.

This is one reason why prior to transitioning from the latent and incipient phase to other phases of an insurgency, the core group attempts to establish an extensive clandestine cellular network, to include training subordinates, before counterinsurgent operations and population control measures can be implemented. This requirement for personal contact for training provides counterinsurgents with an exploitable weakness of clandestine networks— the requirement for freedom of movement. Without freedom of movement, the result of population-control measures that isolate the population from the insurgents, the insurgent leaders are unable to replace, further develop, or grow a clandestinely competent network that has a chance for long-term survival. This explains why the periphery or edge elements, the "low-hanging fruit" of the clandestine organization, may receive little or no clandestine training since these elements can be replaced more easily and with less risk to the network than it would take to train them to be proficient.[243]

Considerations for Elements at the Edge of the Clandestine Organization (Cells and individuals)

Unlike other parts of the clandestine cellular network, the edge elements are generally poorly-trained individuals hired specifically to carry out attacks on the counterinsurgents. By their very nature, these are the highest-risk operations carried out by the clandestine network. If the skills required to conduct these attacks are minimal, then the hiring of less skilled, but more abundant individuals is preferred. The training these individuals or cells receive on clandestine arts will depend solely on how easy they are to replace. The harder to replace, the more time the network leadership will spend to train them to minimize their signature and provide them with some level of protection.

These types of cells and individuals are the true "low-hanging fruit" of a clandestine cellular network and likely consist of individuals that are hired to carry out direct attacks or intelligence collection against the counterinsurgent force. In most cases, these cells consist of individuals that are formed by a cell leader who may or may not have training or experience in clandestine operations. Generally, the cell leader is the only individual that links to the main network through a cut-out, while the rest of the cell communicates amongst themselves. These individuals may simply be in need of money, desire to regain honor by fighting the counterinsurgent directly, or they are not competent enough for higher levels of responsibility within the organization.[244] They are hired to participate with the recognition by the network leadership that they will likely not survive long against competent counterinsurgents. Even with little training, they will cause some disruption in the counterinsurgent activities, but can be quickly replaced by other individuals with similar needs (money, regain honor, et cetera) if or when interdicted.

The only thing that matters to the leader is that there is a solid cut-out between the cell and the clandestine organization. If the leader can replace a cell simply by paying a group of individuals to attack the counterinsurgent force, he can repeat this process indefinitely. There is no incentive to waste time and risk his exposure trying to link-up to train the group in clandestine arts or to expose himself to try to physically reconnect the cell to the network if the cell is interdicted.[245] This is especially pertinent when the cell is responsible for engaging the enemy, either directly with small-arms fire, or indirectly with an explosive device, and thus becomes a priority target of the counterinsurgent.

This attention these edge organizations draw from the counterinsurgent serves an additional purpose, intentionally or not. Simply based on requirements for force protection, the local counterinsurgent force will have the local cells and individuals on their high priority target lists for interdiction.

If the cell is very proficient, then the counterinsurgent may become solely focused on capturing or killing the cell. The proclivity of U.S. and the West counternetwork operations to focus on these kinetic elements of the insurgency provides the true clandestine organization with a built in "security buffer." Thus, the counterinsurgent is focused on the most kinetically active elements of the insurgency, and therefore is unable to focus on the non-kinetic elements of the clandestine cellular network that are of greater danger to the overall COIN effort. In effect, these less-trained and sophisticated elements end up being the primary target of the counterinsurgent.[246] This provides the clandestine cellular network with time and space to provide support to other elements that are achieving the tactical, operational, and strategic objectives of the movement.

Lastly, there is little requirement for emergency reconnection of edge elements when they are interdicted. Even if a cell member manages to evade capture and escapes from or is released by the counterinsurgents, the clandestine leaders must decide if it is worth the risk to reincorporate the individual. Before the leadership conducts procedures for emergency reconnect, the leaders of the clandestine network must trust the individual enough to reincorporate them into the organization. Since these elements are easier to replace, the leadership may decide that the risks for re-incorporating an individual that may be under control or surveillance of the counterinsurgent are too great. In this case, this individual will not be reincorporated or even contacted.

Section Summary

This section described how clandestine networks use function—clandestine art or tradecraft—to minimize signature and thus detection by counterinsurgent forces. The form in this case is functional compartmentalization, which complements the organizational and structural compartmentalization described earlier. Functional compartmentalization refers to the actions of the network members to reduce the signature of the interactions between members. This is done to "hide" the network from the counterinsurgents in order to protect the clandestine cellular network from effective counternetwork operations.

This section analyzed historic examples of different types of clandestine interactions to provide the reader with a deeper understanding of the types of actions that take place in clandestine cellular networks including personal and impersonal communications, how networks reconnect when nodes are removed through counternetwork operations, counter surveillance, and recruiting. This section also discussed how insurgents learn and how they risk the interdiction of the less-trained elements along the edge or periphery of the actual clandestine network to attack the counterinsurgent.

Thus, this section's explanation of functional compartmentalization and signature reduction, along with the previous section on organizational and structural compartmentalization together provide the resilience of the clandestine cellular network. Through both the form and function, the clandestine cellular network is able to ensure its survival, the ultimate logic of the clandestine cellular network.

4. Logic of Clandestine Cellular Networks

From an understanding of the form and function, the logic behind clandestine cellular networks emerges. The main purpose of this organizational form and the way it functions is for long-term survival in order for the movement to reach its political end state. Every aspect of the form, function, and logic is focused on limiting damage from counterinsurgent strikes or making it difficult for the counterinsurgent to find something decisive to strike. It is about balancing the need to conduct operations to gain and maintain support while also protecting the core movement. It is these aspects of clandestine cellular networks that are difficult for Western theorists and practitioners to understand and recognize because they generally do not have a worldview based on the idea of *long-term* or *survival*. The West has grown accustomed to quick conventional wars and has a difficult time understanding how any individual would be willing to live under the strain of a clandestine lifestyle, constantly in fear of being killed or captured, willing to risk everything for a cause, and operating this way for years or even decades. As DA PAM 550-104 explains:

> To fully understand how and why an individual makes certain decisions or takes certain actions, it is essential to understand how he perceives the world around him.... [Individuals] assume roles which are defined by the nature of the organization. For this reason knowledge of underground organization is important and prerequisite to the understanding of the behavior of underground members. When an individual joins a subversive organization, the organization becomes a major part of his daily life and alters his patterns of behavior markedly.[247]

Clandestine cellular networks are also not easy to understand militarily since the whole premise seems conniving, unjust, and subversive, versus the accepted nobility of modern warriors, who practice overt lethal operations. It is the reason Western militaries are drawn to fighting overt guerrillas, and why the current and past doctrinal publications focus so heavily on the counter-guerrilla fight, yet barely mention anything about the underground.[248] Western militaries readily understand overt military units with general hierarchal formations. They do not understand clandestine cellular networks. It is the same reason that the modern ideas of "networks" do not seem to capture the form, function, and logic of insurgent networks. This is why in the absence of understanding, theorists and practitioners alike apply their own understanding of networks based on Western perceptions. Thus, they cognitively force the square peg of "clandestine cellular networks" into the round hole of modern "information-age networks." The logic of clandestine cellular networks is the antithesis to technologically- focused conventional warfare and highly connected information-age networks. Based on this study, the reality of clandestine cellular networks and their form and function presents a very different picture. The final element is the systemic understanding of the logic ensuring the movement's survival in order to achieve its political goals.

Goals and Survival

The overall political goals of the movement are the definite driving force behind the logic of the organization. The successful accomplishment of the goals is partly driven by the strategy, the ideology, or motivation, but ultimately rests on the fact that the organization must survive to reap the benefits of its struggle.[249] Successful accomplishment of the purpose of the insurgency, whether to coerce, disrupt, dissuade, or overthrow a government, or force the withdrawal of an occupying power, rests on its ability to maintain its potential for carrying on the conflict—winning by not losing— which is why the organizational form, function, and logic of clandestine cellular networks matter. It provides a means of keeping the core members alive, regardless of setbacks. The clandestine network will gladly sacrifice the overt elements for the sake of the clandestine element's survival.[250] It will revert to the latent and incipient phase if necessary and will wait for better conditions, which may be months, years, or decades.[251]

Time for the insurgent relates to the desire and motivation for accomplishing the goal, not convenience or impatience. This also separates those insurgents that can be morally and cognitively defeated, generally based on grievances or false motivating factors that prove unreachable, and those that will require killing or capturing, which are generally the ideologically-motivated individuals, driven by religion, culture, or ethnicity. The core may apply other less-overt means of conflict to create space and time to regenerate or strengthen the underground. These measures could include:

- Using overt political wings to attempt to reach the goals through non-violent means, while increasing the strength of overt and clandestine elements in the insurgency if nonviolent means are unsuccessful;
- Ending lethal operations and going completely underground until more favorable conditions exist
- Agreeing with government cease fires in order to buy time to rebuild the organization
- Even reconciling with the government, but demobilizing only the overt elements of the movement, ensuring that the clandestine elements survive to continue the fight in the near future

All of these measures are meant to ensure the key parts of the organization survive to fight for the insurgency another day.

The combination of attaining goals and survival explains the logic that makes insurgencies so difficult to defeat, and why insurgents that use the protracted war theory in conjunction with this logic can wear down a government, an occupier, or a nation-state providing external support to the host nation.[252] This is the same reason insurgencies that use military focused insurgency strategies, better known as Foco—small bands of guerrillas with no infrastructure as inspired by Che Guevera—or insurgencies that have a single charismatic leader, succeed only when the governments they face are incompetent. In these cases, if the government practices counterinsurgency with some competence, they can more easily defeat these movements. In both cases, military-focused movements and movements built around a charismatic leader can be defeated because they lack a solid clandestine cellular network upon which to build, support, and sustain the movement, while simultaneously providing the organization with resilience in the face of setbacks.[253] Conspiratorial insurgencies, on the other hand, are primarily underground, and thus can survive a long time, but may lack the mass—physical, moral, or cognitive—to pose a serious threat in the near and mid-term, unless it is capable of fomenting a mass uprising or conducting a coup d'état.[254]

Israeli military theorist Shimon Naveh provides an interesting and applicable interpretation of goals. He notes that military systems, which are based on their use of violence, loosely describe insurgencies as having two "interaction characteristics." The first matches with the organizational form of a hierarchy with decentralized execution as found in clandestine cellular networks, which Naveh refers to as the "succession of echelonment." This is based on "a deep setting, hierarchal structure and a columnar mode of relation between the system's components, or between sub-systems within the overall system."[255] Second, is "the absolute dominance of the system's [goal]," which as Naveh explains is, "the initial assertion of the [goal] of the system's brain or directing authority predetermines the comprehensive whole, i.e. the all-embracing accomplishment of its future destined action."[256] In this sense, the use of a clandestine cellular network as the organizational form is inherent due to the insatiable desire for organizational survival in order to succeed in its political struggle. This same theory is behind the historic conspiratorial insurgency and shows the amateurish idea of a Foco insurgency as espoused by Che Guevara, which rests entirely on the most vulnerable component of the insurgency--the guerrillas—with its vulnerability due to its overt nature. Although Guevara may have survived the application of his Foco theory in Cuba due to the ineptness of the Batista government, he paid with his life for using it in Bolivia.[257] In Guevara's case, he desired to have his theory launch a greater revolutionary movement in the Third World, but did not link the "logic" of the movement with the correct form and function based on changing circumstances in the countries where he wanted to spread his movement. In Bolivia's case, the Bolivian counterinsurgency effort, with advisory assistance from U.S. Special Forces, was much more competent and capable in finding and defeating Guevara's guerrilla band. The logic drives the function and form of the movement, but it cannot be applied to all situations without modifications to account for different circumstances, threat tactics, terrain, and so forth.

Pressures and Stresses in Clandestine Cellular Networks

In order to understand the logic of clandestine cellular networks, it is imperative to understand the effects on the members of the organization due to the constant physical, moral, and cognitive pressures associated with operating clandestinely. The simple fact that clandestine networks operate under the constant pressure of "death or capture," further delineates clandestine cellular networks from information-age networks.[258] Individuals involved in information-age networks such as the Internet, business, or social networking do not normally operate under the pressure of being killed or captured.[259] They may have pressures such as market share or popularity, which may equate to "survival," but in response, these networks survive by having the largest signature as possible to draw new clients, business contacts, or market share. The pressures on the clandestine individual differ most readily in the fact that members of the organization must practice clandestine arts in every aspect of their lives, or risk death or capture. Author Raymond Momboisse, in his book *Blueprint of Revolution*, provides an interesting summary of the pressure of clandestine life:

> Underground work itself, even if stripped of all danger, is hard work. It must be done meticulously and yet at high speed. But danger cannot be removed; it is an integral part of the way of life and it takes its toll physically and mentally. The pressure is beyond description. The underground worker constantly lives on nerves, as he must, watching his every move, his every word. The work stretches nerves and fatigue stretches them even further, but it is the constant fear that nearly snaps those nerves. The agent cannot let anything go unnoted and unquestioned. He is in a constant state of fear, indeed, he must be, for it works to keep him alive. It maintains the instincts of self-preservation on continuous alert.[260]

When they fail to practice the clandestine arts or establish their networks in accordance with a secure organizational form, they begin to have an increased signature which the counterinsurgents can exploit.

Complacency, laziness, and overconfidence of network leaders or members are all exploitable elements of human nature. It is the individuals who practice solid clandestine art that survive, but they pay a price due to the constant pressures they live under which includes:

- Paranoia of being constantly followed or under surveillance
- Fear of compromise by infiltrators or spies, which leads to distrust
- Requirements of clandestine lifestyles, such as constantly changing locations to remain safe from counterinsurgent raids or strikes
- Not having direct control of subordinates nor having direct contact with superiors
- Needing tactical, operational and strategic patience due to the slow responsiveness of clandestine networks as information is passed up and down the network clandestinely

The pressure also mounts as network members are killed or captured, especially for the superior or subordinate of these individuals.[261] Depending on the experience level of the leaders and members, the removal of individual nodes within the network, or cells that are on the edge of the organization, may or may not cause an increase in pressure. Generally, in an experienced network with solid organizational and functional compartmentalization and practices, single nodes or periphery cells being killed or captured is expected and well within the tolerance levels of the network. While disconcerting, it is not demoralizing. Seasoned clandestine operators overcome some of this anxiety by trusting that the form and function that protect them and the network are still sound.

Additionally, and often overlooked, is the fact that experience and confidence increases for those individuals unfortunate enough to get detained, questioned, and even imprisoned, but eventually released. By having exposure to the interworking of the counterinsurgents detention processes, the network members gain a new level of understanding of the inner workings of the counterinsurgents' methods that they can then use to educate their organization. For those who get the opportunity to intermingle with other detainees, it provides the additional opportunity to make contacts and gain additional knowledge on how other networks are operating. The counterinsurgency practice of detaining members of a network but releasing them prior to the defeat of the network, commonly referred to as "catch and release programs," makes the organization stronger and more confident.[262] They begin to learn and adapt to the counterinsurgent tactical operations and detention processes.[263] This increases the confidence of the network leaders and allows lessons learned to be passed to less-experienced members to mentally prepare them for similar experiences. It also provides the leaders with decision points on warning other network members of the individual's detention if there is a chance of compromise to other parts of the network.

Finally, and another often overlooked result of regular exposure to counterinsurgent and counternetwork operations is that the counterinsurgents begin to establish discernible patterns. This is especially problematic when the counterinsurgents use the same tactics, techniques, and procedures against individuals in the same network. The insurgents continue to learn from each interaction with the counterinsurgents and are always looking for weaknesses or patterns that they can exploit. This includes developing patterns of indicators and early warning of potential counterinsurgency or counternetwork operations, and more importantly, the realization of the type of intelligence the counterinsurgent is using to make decisions on when and who to target. Examples of questions that the network leaders and members might ask themselves after any type of attack on the network may include: How did this happen? How did the counterinsurgents find the member? What was he doing when he was detained or killed? Who knew he was at the location? Were there any odd occurrences before the attack? And, what new tactic, technique, or procedures did the counterinsurgent use in executing this strike?[264] All are pertinent questions that may expose an organizational vulnerability that requires the network to adapt.

This knowledge also allows the clandestine cellular network leaders to develop counter tactics, to include providing false targeting information to deceive or to bait the counterinsurgents into a position of disadvantage. When the insurgent is able to turn the tables on the counterinsurgent by using the counterinsurgent's own tactics, techniques, and procedures against them, then the insurgents have the initiative. With the initiative comes increased confidence and reduced stress since the insurgents are dictating the counterinsurgent's actions.

Section Summary

This section described the logic of clandestine cellular networks—long-term survival—which requires the form and function of the networks to guarantee. As this section explained, it is the main purpose of the organizational form and function to reduce the risk of detection and compromise that may lead to organizational defeat prior to the realization of the movement's political end state. The aspects of form and function all work together to ensure the viability of the clandestine cellular network, and ultimately the movement.

This section further describes the difficulties of living the life as a clandestine operator. The stresses the individual feels subside with experience. Analysis of the form, function, and the logic provides a set of principles for clandestine cellular networks, presented in the next section.

5. The Principles of Clandestine Cellular Networks

Based on an analysis of the form, function, and logic of clandestine cellular networks, the survival of a clandestine organization rests on six principles (see Figure 11): compartmentalization, resilience, low signature, purposeful growth, operational risk, and organizational learning. These six principles can be used by the counterinsurgent to analyze current network theories, doctrine, and clandestine adversaries to identify strengths and weaknesses.

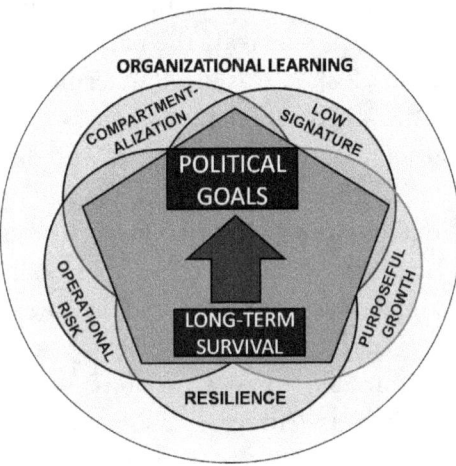

Figure 13. Principles of Clandestine Cellular Networks[265]

First, *compartmentalization* comes both from form and function and protects the organization by reducing the number of individuals with direct knowledge of other members, plans, and operations. Compartmentalization provides the proverbial wall to counter counterinsurgent exploitation and intelligence driven operations. Second, *resilience* comes from organizational form and functional compartmentalization, which not only minimizes damage due to counterinsurgency strikes on the network, but also provides a functional method for reconnecting the network around individuals (nodes) that have been killed or captured. Third is *low signature*, a functional component based on the application of clandestine art or tradecraft, which minimize the signature of communications, movement, inter-network interaction, and operations of the network. *Purposeful growth* is the fourth principle, highlighting the fact that these types of networks do not grow in accordance to modern information network theories, but grow with purpose or aim—to gain access to a target, sanctuary, population, intelligence, or resources.[266] Purposeful growth primarily relies on clandestine means of recruiting new members based on the overall purpose of the network, branch, or cell.

The fifth principle is *operational risk*, which stresses the clandestine paradox between conducting operations to gain or maintain influence, relevance, or reach in order to attain the political goals and long-term survival of the movement.[267] Operations increase the observable signature of the organization, threatening its survival. The paradox comes in balancing the risk—winning by not losing. It is in these terms that the clandestine cellular networks of the underground develop overt fighting forces—rural and urban—to lethally and non-lethally interact with the target audiences: the population, the government, the international community, and third party countries conducting foreign internal defense in support of the government forces.[268] This is done to gain moral, physical, and/or cognitive advantage over the counterinsurgent forces and the government by increasing the popular internal support for the movement, as well gain or maintain external support from third party nations or non-state actors. This interaction invariably leads to increased observable signature and counternetwork operations against the insurgent overt elements. However, to balance the paradox of operational risk, these overt elements can rebuild given time and resources. What cannot be rebuilt are the core members, the driving force behind the insurgency. These elements stay alive by taking care not to emit any signature that can be detected by the counterinsurgent unless necessary, and making sure they are compartmented from each other should one be detected.

Lastly, *organizational learning*, the sixth principle, is the fundamental need to learn and adapt the clandestine cellular network to:

- The current situation
- The threat environment
- The overall organizational goals and strategy
- The relationship with the external support mechanisms
- The changing tactics, techniques, and procedures of the counterinsurgents

- Technology
- Terrain—physical, human, and cyber

Although the insurgent core and network leaders and members must continually adapt and learn based on these factors, one of the most important clandestine principles is to learn and adapt based on successes and failures of the form, function, and logic of the clandestine cellular network.[269] Understanding, learning, and adapting to the factors above allows for the clandestine cellular network to become stronger and more proficient.

Thus, much of the logic of clandestine cellular networks emerges from these six principles, and all evolve around the often repeated adage, "insurgents win by not losing." It is for this reason that survival of the movement's core members, or other highly dedicated members who will carry on the fight even if the core is lost, is imperative. These members must remain largely under the counterinsurgent radar by applying the form, function, and logic of clandestine cellular networks for long-term survival. The insurgents may lose the conventional battle, including all of their overt force, but the organization can and will rebuild upon its core, even if it has to wait for a long period of time for the right conditions to reemerge. Insurgent time and Western time are not comparable, nor are the insurgent and Western ideas of defeat.

Defeat of a conventional fighting force in the past may have meant victory, but for an insurgency, the defeat of its overt forces equates to only a setback.[270] Defeat against an insurgency also does not come simply by securing the population, as U.S. doctrine promotes, although this is the first step.[271] The other steps that must take place include isolating the clandestine networks from external support, and isolating the reconcilable insurgents from the irreconcilables. Until these conditions are satisfactorily met, the fight will continue, maybe not overtly, with subversion and terrorism once again emerging as the primary methods of the latent-and-incipient phase, but it will continue, especially for ideologically motivated individuals. Victory comes for the counterinsurgent only when there are no more irreconcilables, either through turning them, completely isolating and thus marginalizing them, capturing and long-term detention, or killing them. This is the only way to truly overcome the form, function, and logic to gain victory against the insurgents. However, if the insurgents successfully apply the principles of clandestine cellular networks, then their ability to survive is fundamental to the eventual realization of the movement's political goals.

6. Conclusion and Recommendations

> In seeking a solution, it is essential to realize that in modern warfare we are not up against just a few armed bands spread across a given territory, but rather against an armed clandestine organization whose essential role is to impose its will upon the population. Victory will be obtained only through the complete destruction of that organization. This is the master concept that must guide us in our study of modern warfare. —Roger Trinquier (1964)[272]

Conclusion

Although each insurgency is unique, underground clandestine cellular networks as the foundation of insurgent organizations are not, nor are their form, function, and logic. Since the dawn of society, clandestine cellular networks have been used to hide nefarious activities within the human terrain. While there has been an increased interest in the use of these types of networks since 9/11, few network theorists or counternetwork theorists and practitioners understand that these networks have a peculiar organizational form, function, and logic. The wrong ontology and epistemology, largely based on mirror-imaging information-age network theories onto clandestine cellular networks, have led many network and counternetwork theorists astray. Most theorists and practitioners cognitively mirror information-age networks to clandestine cellular networks, which, as this monograph has shown, is largely incorrect. Failure to understand the aspects of clandestine cellular networks has huge implications to both the way network theorists study and model networks, as well as how network attack theorists recommend defeating clandestine cellular networks. This misunderstanding is due to the lack of appreciation for the form, function, and logic of clandestine cellular networks, and ultimately the importance of "organization," one of the seven dynamics of insurgency.

Within the seven dynamics of insurgency, theoretical and doctrinal understanding of the organization has been largely focused on the overt military elements of the insurgency, the guerrillas. Throughout history, guerrillas, or the overt military elements of an insurgency, have generally been a rural component, supported by clandestine urban and support components, like the underground and auxiliary, both of which remained largely hidden. For the West, it is easier to understand and identify with the overt military elements since they are generally organized along commonly understood military hierarchical formations and use basic infantry-type tactics. This is not the case with clandestine elements of an insurgency that require understanding of the form, function, and logic, along with patience and the discriminate use of force, to capture or kill through counternetwork operations.

As the world's societies have migrated into the urban areas, the urban guerrilla, underground, and auxiliaries, all operating as clandestine cellular networks, have become increasingly important. This trend will only increase as urbanization increases, providing the "urban jungle" in which these clandestine cellular networks will find refuge and thrive in the future. The problem from a Western military perspective and for the counterinsurgent is that the underground and auxiliary elements exist amongst the people. This fact frustrates the counterinsurgent operations due to their proximity to the center of gravity for both the insurgent and counterinsurgent—the people. Any misapplication of force by the counterinsurgent automatically delegitimizes the government's efforts. Thus, the ability of the clandestine cellular networks to blend with the human terrain increases the difficulty of the counternetwork operations.

To further compound this paradox is the lack of theoretical, doctrinal, and operational understanding of the form, function, and logic of clandestine cellular networks. Since 9/11, counternetwork operations have been based on widely accepted information-age network theories. These theories have resulted in counternetwork operations focused on attacking key nodes and hubs within the network in an effort to disconnect the network. Although these theories seem intuitive, a deeper understanding of the form, function, and logic of clandestine cellular networks reveals that these networks have little in common with

Figure 14. An Afghan man detained as a suspected insurgent by Afghan and Canadian troops is led away with his hands bound in the village of Salavat in the insurgent stronghold of Panjwaii District. Photo used by permission of Newscom.

information-age networks. By incorrectly focusing on the removal of single high-value targets or highly-connected individuals, counternetwork operations since 9/11 have operated within the tolerance level of most clandestine cellular networks.

The form, function, and logic construct allows for a greater understanding of clandestine cellular networks and the correct application of counternetwork operations. First, form explains the development and interaction of the organizational components of the insurgency—the guerrillas, underground, and auxiliary—specifically focusing on the clandestine components. Further analysis of the clandestine cellular elements reveals that historically, these elements have made up the largest portions of the overall insurgent organization. This monograph also showed that this relationship can be explained in much the same way as conventional military tooth-to-tail ratios, with the guerrilla elements making up only a fraction of the insurgency in comparison to the clandestine elements. This understanding further revealed the overall historical scale of the clandestine networks, based on ideas of network leaders and sub-leaders recruiting and developing their subordinates.

The investigation of the organizational form also revealed compartmented elements built upon the foundation of the cell. Cells are connected via links to leaders that form branches, sub-networks, and ultimately networks, each with its own function or set of functions. Separating these cells, branches, sub-networks, and networks is a method of structure compartmentalization. One method is the so-called cut-out which ensures there is no direct link between two individuals. The other common method is ensuring that mission essential information is only shared on a need-to-know basis. Compartmentalization ultimately protects the organization by limiting the damage done by a counterinsurgent operation should a member of the network be detained or killed. The better the structural compartmentalization, the more effectively damage will be limited. The counterinsurgent's ability to exploit poor compartmentalization by tracing the direct linkages from one individual, cell, or network to another will effectively end at the cut-out if established correctly. If the cut-out is not properly established, then the counternetwork operations may result in catastrophic failure of the compartmentalization.

Second is the organizational function of the clandestine cellular network, which relies on the application of clandestine arts or tradecraft to lower the signature of the member interaction and operations of the network. This is done to allow the network to maintain the lowest signature possible in order to deny the counterinsurgent an aspect of the clandestine cellular network to conduct counternetwork operations against. Clandestine art is also applied to minimize the interaction of network members as they pass information or instructions, reconnect the network after a member has been killed or captured, and to recruit new members to replace losses or to grow. Clandestine recruiting is another clandestine function that is required to gain access to additional logistics and political support or into target areas. In this case, the clandestine recruiting is used to grow the organization purposefully rather than haphazardly. It is only with regard to the edge organizations, such as the operational cells, that are at high risk for interdiction. The clandestine leader assumes this risk based on his trust of the form and function of his network, assuming that he has enough safe guards in place to remain undetected, even as he establishes, trains, and if required, replaces lost cells. Regardless of the precautions or where members interact within the organization, all interactions are high-risk endeavors. They require the solid application of clandestine art or tradecraft to ensure the core members are not detected and interdicted by the counterinsurgents.

Last is the overall logic of clandestine cellular networks. This ultimately centers on the movement's long-term survival in an effort to reach its political goals; in other words, winning by not losing. The overall purpose of the insurgent movement is long-term survival, relying on the form, function, and logic of clandestine cellular networks to first, minimize the signature of the network to make it difficult for the counterinsurgent to detect, and second, if detected and attacked by the counterinsurgent, to limit the damage. It is also about balancing the need for long-term survival to reach the political goal, while ensuring that the insurgency is active enough to gain or maintain popular internal support and external support. This study has also shown the logic of these networks is based on a worldview where time is relative to the objectives the insurgency seeks, with some core

> *...time is relative to the objectives the insurgency seeks, with some core members willing to pursue goals for years and even decades while constantly under the pressure of being killed or captured.*

members willing to pursue goals for years and even decades while constantly under the pressure of being killed or captured.

As this monograph explains, it is the clandestine cellular networks that ensure long-term survival of the organization, not the overt military elements against which Western militaries routinely and historically have focused their COIN fight. This overt element made up of guerrillas is one tool of the insurgency, but one that given enough time can be replaced if defeated or destroyed. What cannot be replaced is the core movement, those individuals who established the initial movement and will carry on the fight despite setbacks, willing to revert to previous phases of the insurgency if required. It is these individuals that can wait for better conditions, even if it means waiting for decades. This analysis further explained this point by comparing protracted war, military-focused, and conspiratorial insurgency theories. Clandestine cellular networks play a significant role in all but the Foco theory, which is an indicator of the non-viability of this theory given a competent counterinsurgent force and government.

In analyzing the logic, the pressures and stresses of living the clandestine lifestyle were also studied. The pressures of living under constant fear of being killed or captured further separate clandestine cellular networks from information-age networks, such as social and business networking. The pressures alone force the clandestine operators to constantly worry about their application of the form and functions of clandestine cellular networks, a worry that most information-age network members do not face. Ultimately successful counternetwork operations rest on the ability to force the core members to make mistakes by pushing them out of their comfort zones and into carrying out an action that is detectable by the counterinsurgent. This can only be done when the counternetwork operations overcome the form, function, and logic of the network.

Lastly, six clandestine cellular network principles emerged from the analysis of this study, capturing the essence of the form, function, and logic, and centered on long-term movement survival—compartmentalization, resilience, low signature, purposeful growth, operational risk, and organizational learning. These six principles provide a method for testing network theories for feasibility, acceptability, and suitability. It provides a model for exposing the counterinsurgent to the understanding of the critical elements of the insurgency, the clandestine cellular networks, as the first step in developing effective counternetwork operations.

Recommendations

First, the U.S. military needs to conduct further research into the form, function, and logic of contemporary insurgencies, specifically those in Iraq, Afghanistan, and globally, focused on al-Qaeda and its associated movements. These studies should use the Special Operations Research Office products from the 1960s as a model for these efforts. The author recommends deploying researchers to Iraq and Afghanistan to interview former Sunni and Shi'a insurgents, such as the members of the Sons of Iraq, and detained insurgents, in order to develop an in-depth understanding of the local, as well as al-Qaeda and Iranian, methods of clandestine cellular network operations.

Second, include a detailed discussion of the form, function, and logic of clandestine cellular networks in the future version of both the FM 3-24 and JP 3-24. The purpose of this recommendation is to increase the understanding of this organizational form amongst the joint force. Until the joint force completely understands this aspect of insurgent movements, successful counterinsurgency will be difficult, if not impossible to achieve.

Third, conduct comparative analysis of the form, function, and logic of clandestine cellular networks with current network and network attack methodologies to identify which network theories and network attack methodologies are truly feasible, acceptable, and suitable. Adjust current counternetwork operations—tactically, operationally, and strategically—based on this analysis, and include in the future versions of FM 3-24 and JP 3-24. Successful counternetwork operations by the joint forces will require a full understanding of the form, function, and logic of the clandestine cellular networks, or the joint force is likely to continue to apply incorrect counternetwork methodologies. This will not lead to the defeat of our networked adversaries, but will lead to exhaustion of the joint force, and the ultimate goal of insurgent movements, the exhaustion of national will to support partners and allies faced with insurgencies.

Last, the joint force should shift from target lists based on high value individuals or highly connected individuals, to target lists based on priority networks. It's the grouping of individuals in networks that must be addressed, not the individuals themselves that matter. Once the targeting efforts shift from individual to network focus, the counternetwork operations will begin to more fully realize methods for overcoming the form, function, and logic. This includes counternetwork operations against all of the individuals in the network near-simultaneously to overcome the ability of the network to adapt to single individuals being removed. Simultaneous attacks will further stress the ability of the networks to conduct clandestine functions, such as reconnecting the network around lost nodes. If a large amount of nodes are removed at one time, then the network will be in disarray. Finally, these types of large-scale operations against the networks will begin to attack the logic of the insurgency, force it to either return to the latent and incipient phase, or face destruction.

The correct application of counternetwork operations based on understanding the form, function, and logic of the clandestine cellular networks will provide the opportunity to gain space and time for the political aspects of the counterinsurgency strategy to be applied. It is the political aspects that solve root causes of insurgency. Military action can only be used to secure the populace, isolate the insurgents from internal and external support, and provide the host nation government with the opportunity to regain the legitimacy to govern the entire population. ⬆

Appendix A – Types of Clandestine Cellular Networks

Based on the form, function, and the previous elements of logic—goals, decision making, and principles—different types of clandestine cellular networks emerge that are not clearly captured in the form, function, and logic context, but are important to the overall understanding of clandestine cellular networks. This monograph focused on the use of clandestine cellular networks within the framework of an insurgency, both interstate and globally. Three distinguishing aspects of types of clandestine cellular networks are evident: professional (trained) or non-professional (on-the-job training), indigenous (internal) or non-indigenous (external support), and then network typologies that do not fit these categories—non-state actors conducting global insurgency and closed-network special purpose operations of limited scope. These specific classifications of clandestine cellular networks are largely overlooked or misunderstood by theorists and doctrine. However, there are huge implications related to clearly defining the threat. Identifying the proficiency of the members of the network allows the counterinsurgents to better understand the form, function, and logic of a given network, to include the network's likely strengths and weaknesses, which is critical to effective targeting.

"Professional" is loosely defined as an individual having some formalized training in conducting clandestine arts or tradecraft, while the non-professional has learned the trade through on-the-job training or an evolutionary process—in a sense, "survival of the fittest." This taxonomy also includes a contrast in clandestine capability between the insurgents, which by definition are indigenous to a country, and members of a clandestine, non-indigenous, external support network, either a nation-state or non-state actors. Obviously, nation-states have capabilities to conduct espionage against rivals, as well as establishing specially-trained intelligence or military special operations forces to conduct training, advising, and equipping of insurgencies against rivals as another tool of diplomacy. Although the espionage operations have always been clandestine in nature, the requirement to use clandestine cellular networks to support the insurgency has increased with urbanization in some countries, such as Iran and its Intelligence Services and the Iranian Revolutionary Guard Corps efforts against the U.S. in Iraq as a good example of this growing trend.

Non-state actors have now emerged as another type of external support, but to date have largely been confused with the indigenous insurgent elements. Arguably, al-Qaeda is the current "gold standard" of non-state actors that use clandestine cellular networks to link like-minded interstate insurgencies with its global insurgent clandestine cellular network. Al-Qaeda, as an example, can also be further subdivided into the overall global insurgency movement and special-purpose networks, such as financial networks, intelligence networks, logistics support, and strategic attack networks, such as the closed network that carried out the 9/11 attacks. Thus, the six subcategories of clandestine cellular networks that emerge are: internal non-professional, internal professional, external professional, external non-professional, non-state clandestine networks, and non-state special purpose cells and networks. These will be explained in detail below.

Internal Clandestine Cellular Networks (Non-Professional and Professional)

First, internal non-professional clandestine cellular networks consist of insurgents with no formal clandestine training, which is indicative of the grass roots type of insurgency. The non-professionals learn largely from surviving their mistakes or adapting based on their observations of others' successes or failures. There is also the possibility that they have access to military-like training manuals or the Internet, providing them access to the theory of clandestine operations. The top tier of this category are those individuals who have received some type of informal clandestine training from nation-state intelligence, military, or law-enforcement members, likely as an agent of these individuals to gather intelligence. Given these skills, this tier of non-professionals have a distinct advantage and better potential for success through the application of their training to keep the signature of their organization low as it develops and grows.

There is a subset of this first type routinely described as "leaderless jihadists," who start their own grassroots movements based on the ideology of a larger organization, but to which they do not have direct links. As Robert Martinage explains, "Over the past several years, a number of individuals, with distant or no links to al-Qaeda and scant terrorist training, have responded to its call to defensive jihad against the West. Inspired by a common cause, these individuals coalesce for a limited campaign or even a single operation." Second, individuals with some type of formal training in clandestine operations, generally from the intelligence, military, or law enforcement communities, develop internal professional clandestine cellular networks. Having likely been trusted members of the former regime, these types of clandestine operators largely emerge after an authoritarian regime has been overthrown, such as the so-called "former-regime elements" in Iraq. Due to their positions within the security apparatus prior to the overthrow, they likely are still loyal to the previous regime. Thus, they apply their clandestine skills to counter those responsible for the overthrow. Although beyond the scope of this monograph, this is an important consideration when a regime removal becomes an option for the U.S. and can be termed as a country's "clandestine potential" referring to the built-in capacity for the population and security apparatus to use their clandestine skills to develop a large, but hidden clandestine cellular network. These elements could include former military, intelligence, or law-enforcement personnel who were trained by the government.

External Clandestine Cellular Networks (Non-Professional and Professional)

The next two types of networks are both external support networks; one is a nation-state network, made up of intelligence or specially trained military personnel, and the other is a non-state actor network. Both have certain commonalities that must be understood first. Nation-states or non-state actors provide support for insurgency, also known as unconventional warfare, as a low-cost, low-risk, economy of force capability to put pressure on an adversary nation indirectly without having to resort to conventional military methods. Historically, external support provides the insurgency with an increased likelihood of success. There are three types of external support—indirect, direct, and combat. Indirect support consists of political recognition, economic or information support, training outside of the conflict area, or support provided through a third party nation. Direct support would include the previous, but with a more direct relationship, including providing advisors to train, equip, and advise the insurgency, short of combat, and most likely conducted in a sanctuary or liberated area near or within the state in conflict, respectively. Lastly, combat support would include all of the previously mentioned types of support, but advisors would work directly with the insurgency within the zone of conflict, accepting the risks associated with this type of interaction and proximity or even direct conflict with the counterinsurgents.[273] During Operation Iraqi Freedom, U.S. and coalition forces faced two external support entities, the nation-state of Iran, providing indirect and direct support to the Shi'a insurgency, and al-Qaeda, a non-state actor, providing indirect, direct, and combat support to the Sunni insurgency, highlighting the differences between the two external support networks—external non-professional and external professional.

External non-professional clandestine cellular networks (ENP-CCN), the third type of clandestine cellular network is inherently defined as members of a non-state actor, like al-Qaeda, which provide support to an insurgency, also known as unconventional warfare.[274] Throughout the conflict in Iraq and Afghanistan, this category was referred to as "foreign fighters and terror-ists," which is a poor descriptor since this category describes foreign entities, but fails to capture the purpose of their actions in support of the insurgency. Despite their obvious foreign origins, they are routinely lumped together with the insurgency, which makes it difficult for the counterinsurgent to understand the nuance of external support, nor the strategy for isolating the insurgents and population from these external actors. Zarqawi and his replacement, Abu Ayyub Al-Masri, are examples of this external non-professional genre. These groups function much like the U.S. Army Special Forces conducting unconventional warfare, providing indirect, direct, or combat support to the insurgency to include training, equipping, fund-ing, as well as advising the insurgent leaders, and if necessary, leading the insurgency.[275] Al-Qaeda in Iraq is a good example of external support gone bad, having suffered from catastrophic loss of rapport with many Sunni insurgent groups and the Sunni population in 2007. Zarqawi also received harsh criticism from the al-Qaeda core, primarily Ayman al-Zawahiri in 2004, for his attacks on the Shi'a population, showing the fine balance that these external support networks must face.

Indirectly, Zarqawi's efforts led to the establishment of recruiting capa-bilities outside the zone of conflict, and then clandestinely infiltrating these individuals, also referred to as "foreign fighters," using clandestine routes or "rat lines" from Europe and the Middle East into Iraq. Rather than being leaders or advisors to the insurgency, these individuals are largely used by AQ cadres as suicide bombers, a method of non-state precision attack, more appropriately described as the jihadi direct attack munitions, a low-technology equivalent to the U.S. joint direct attack munitions, a global positioning system-guided precision munition. The support networks that infiltrate these individuals and provide support to the al-Qaeda elements in Iraq, whether financial or even within the information realm by running al-Qaeda websites, including providing cyber-based training materials, are all part of the indirect support provided by the external, non-professional network. These networks support the Sunni indigenous networks directly through finances, training, advising, and when necessary organizing and leading. This is generally the role Zarqawi had, not participating directly in combat, but more at the managerial level, working with the leaders of the various insurgent groups to gain consensus and unity of effort. His subordinates provided support to local insurgent movements on a regular basis, and provided training, equipment, finances, advisory assistance, and leadership at that level, which included supporting these indigenous units when they engaged in combat. Understanding this allows the counterinsurgency to focus on cutting off external support to deny the insurgents the resources, training, advice, and even leadership, provided by these external support networks. The "external non-professional" categorization applies only within the context of interstate insurgency. The clandestine potential of these advisors varies from very good to very poor depending largely on how they were trained.

The fourth type of clandestine cellular network is a nation-state's external support networks made up of intelligence personnel and/or special operations forces referred to here as external professional clandestine cellular networks. This type of support has taken place throughout history. During Napoleon's conquest of Spain between 1808 and 1814, in which the term "guerrilla" was first coined, Napoleon's forces encountered an insurgency supported by the British. Even earlier than this, the British supported the Calabrian brigands in Southern Italy against Napoleon between 1806 and 1811. External support to insurgencies, especially with respect to large numbers of clandestine cellular external support networks, reached its peak during World War II when the British Special Operations Executive and the American Office of Strategic Services provided the largest clandestine efforts in history to support resistance movements throughout occupied Europe and Asia. During the Cold War, external support to insurgency was the primary method of conflict for the super powers, with the Soviet Union and the U.S. both supporting insurgencies throughout the world in attempt to limit the other superpower's influence in the region. The U.S. faced an

Iran-backed insurgency in Iraq, where Iran covertly supported the Shi'a by providing training, funding, and providing lethal aid, largely used to target U.S. forces and force their withdrawal.

Special Types of Clandestine Cellular Networks for Non-State Actors with Global Reach

The larger clandestine cellular network of al-Qaeda, the global insurgency, and other non-state actors can simply be described as non-state, non-professional clandestine cellular network (NS-NP-CCN), a fifth category. The difference between this network type and the external non-professional type is in its scale and location. The previous typologies were linked to an interstate insurgency and the insurgents and external support networks. This special category, the non-state, non-professional refers to the larger al-Qaeda global insurgency movement. Thus, in one sense, AQ by itself fits the NS-NP-CCN typology, but from a different point of analysis focused on external support to an insurgency, AQ would be categorized as previously mentioned, ENP-CCN. The application of these typologies by the analyst must be based on the problem being solved—a non-state actor as a global insurgency or a non-state actor providing external support to an insurgency.

Additionally, a study of al-Qaeda reveals that not only is it a global insurgency that uses and externally supports like-minded insurgencies to further its cause, it also uses special-purpose cells and networks to conduct strategic, direct-action operations against its "near and far enemies." This requires a sixth, and final category—non-state, special-purpose clandestine cellular networks—the so-called "terrorist cells and network." The 9/11 hijackers and their support network—a closed system—fits this classification perfectly. Other examples include the cells and networks that carried out the attacks against the USS Cole (2000), the Tanzania and Nairobi Embassy bombings (1998), and the Mumbai attacks (2008). Although clearly terrorist acts, the "terrorists" themselves were really specially selected and trained individuals chosen for these operations. This is very similar to the way a nation-state would choose a special operations unit to conduct a specific, compartmented operation of specific purpose. Networks and cells of this type are generally hand-picked by their core-leadership to conduct intelligence gathering, logistics and support operations, and ultimately direct-action operations—terrorist acts, ambushes, raids, murder, and hostage taking. What makes these cells different is not only their focused purpose, but also that they are closed networks, which means that they generally are not adding new members.

Although these types of networks may fluctuate in size, they are generally not growing like other networks since they have a predetermined mission, which requires certain skills, logistics support, and intelligence preparation. It is likely that as the mission or network leaders identify a need for special skills or additional support, those elements can be added; these additions are known and trusted individuals that may or may not know the overall plan. These special-purpose networks and cells are specifically trained, funded, and supported for a certain target. Their mission cycle follows a general pattern of identifying a target that meets the overall effect sought by the core leadership, then developing the intelligence for the target, establishing the support infrastructure for the mission, attacking the target, and lastly, collapsing the intelligence and support networks once the operation is complete to protect the members for future use. Due to their closed nature, it is very difficult for law enforcement to identify these networks unless they make mistakes that raise their signature. However, if this breach happens, law enforcement has generally been very successful at dismantling these operations quickly. The logic of these clandestine cellular networks is different than other categories, since this is a very mission-focused group that relies heavily on form and function for protection due to the fact that they are operating within a foreign environment. If security forces breach the compartmentalized and closed network, the entire network is usually exposed and arrested. Members who escape have to assume that the mission is compromised, and thus cancelled due to the increased risk, resulting in mission failure.

Appendix B - Clandestine Potential

Complex insurgencies, such as in Iraq and Afghanistan, consist of a mixture of clandestine cellular networks and their overt elements. Although understanding the types of networks present in an active insurgency informs the development of effective counternetwork operations, this same knowledge can inform planners on the types of insurgent threats that may emerge due to U.S. military operations in the future, such as the insurgencies encountered as part of Operation Enduring Freedom and Operation Iraqi Freedom. For this monograph, the capability of an insurgency, both inherent and when supported by external entities, is referred to as *clandestine potential*. This potential is derived by the "type" of networks as explained in Appendix A—internal or external, professional or non-professional. Each type determines the overall likelihood that the insurgent movement will be able to successfully build a core group, underground, and auxiliary, without disruption, upon which is built the overt guerrilla units.

The *clandestine potential* is determined by the network members' experiences, society, and culture, as well as external support capabilities provided by a nation-state or non-state actor in the form of training, advising, and providing resources to increase this potential. Thus, an insurgent movement with members who were former intelligence or military officers trained in the clandestine arts would have a greater *clandestine potential* to develop a successful clandestine cellular network than a movement made up of untrained amateurs who simply take up a cause and learn to operate clandestinely through evolutionary growth based on trial and error, much like on-the-job training. So experientially, school-trained individuals of a nation-state's intelligence or military forces would have the requisite skills to clandestinely link into a core of individuals and begin to grow a clandestine organization, as well as having the understanding on how to apply the principles of clandestine operations to different physical, human, and security environments.

In societies largely controlled by the government through the use of internal, human-intelligence collection networks, as found in authoritarian regimes like Saddam Hussein's, there would also be substantial *clandestine potential*. In this example, even within a family, members may be intelligence collectors for the government, yet due to their clandestine ability, the family has no idea that they are passing information to an internal security handler. These same skills, as explained in form and function sections in the monograph, apply readily to all clandestine operations, including establishing an insurgency. This potential is further increased if the regime, with its professional intelligence and military elements, has garnered contacts in other sympathetic nations and can leverage these contacts immediately after being overthrown to provide depth and sanctuaries in other countries, further exacerbating the counterinsurgents' difficulties. A regime worried of being overthrown may also establish plans for using insurgency as a method of regaining power. Thus, comparing counterinsurgency efforts in Iraq with those in Afghanistan based on clandestine potential, the U.S. military could have identified the clandestine potential in Iraq as a significant threat in the post-conflict operations versus those in Afghanistan. Continuing the Iraq example, if this had been identified as an issue, one of the initial tasks would have been to use population-control measures to limit movement and disrupt the ability of these networks from contacting each other clandestinely and developing an underground organization. These networks could also have been attacked early in their underground development as intelligence became available to further disrupt or neutralize their efforts before they were able to move into the guerrilla warfare phase, thus keeping them in a latent or incipient phase of insurgency.

In a country that lacks inherent potential, a third party nation-state or non-state actor may be able to provide training, advising, and equipping either directly, indirectly, or in a combat role to increase the *clandestine potential*. Normally, this would be difficult and would likely take a long time based on just small special operations teams or individual intelligence agents slowly increasing the potential over time, as well as organizing a disparate insurgency by providing a liaison and establishing relationships between disparate groups being advised by the external support mechanism. However, there is another method for a nation- or non-nation-state to rapidly increase the *clandestine potential* by infiltrating large numbers of intelligence or military members, or diasporas who have been selected and trained in clandestine operations and conducting insurgency. If they have links to the target country, they are readily accepted back into their homeland, especially at the end of a crisis.

Examples of this external effort to increase the clandestine potential is the Vietminh cadres left behind by the North Vietnamese government at the end of the Indochina War as well as efforts by Iran to introduce forces, such as the Badr Corps, and Shi'a-Iraqis who had sought refuge in Iran for years prior to the U.S. liberation of Iraq. In the first case, the Vietminh were able to take advantage of the political situation to ensure cadres were left behind or infiltrated back into South Vietnam in the late 1950s and early 1960s to set conditions for the ensuing insurgency that the U.S. and South Vietnam faced throughout the Vietnam War. In the second case, and yet to be studied in depth, Iran infiltrated the Badr Corps into Iraq under the auspices that this force was made up of former Iraqis who Iran hoped would be viewed as liberators, not as Iranian proxies, despite the fact that this unit had long been supported and developed by Iran. This large, well-trained force was infiltrated into key Shi'a areas following the overthrow of Saddam to boost the "clandestine potential" of those areas that did not readily have networks or the know-how to set their own networks. This effort increased the capabilities and clandestine potential over a series of months and years.

Endnotes

1. Derek Jones, *Understanding the Form, Function, and Logic of Clandestine Cellular Networks: The First Step in Effective Counternetwork Operations*, (Ft. Leavenworth, KS: School of Advanced Military Studies, 2009), http://cgsc.cdmhost.com/cdm/ singleitem/collection/p4013coll3/id/2439/rec/1 [accessed August 1, 2011].

2. The author would like to especially thank Jon Wiley, Carrie Worth, Todd Vajner, Daveed Gartenstein-Ross, and JSOU's William Knarr and Anna-Marie Wyant for their time and effort editing and commenting on this version of the text.

3. David Kilcullen, *The Accidental Guerrilla: Fighting Small Wars in the Midst of a Big One*, (New York: Oxford University Press, Inc., 2009), xv; see also Gian Gentile, "A Strategy of Tactics: Population-centric COIN and the Army," *Parameters* (Autumn 2009), http://www.carlisle.army.mil/usawc/Parameters/ Articles/09autumn/gentile.pdf [accessed October 20, 2011], 5-8; Nathan Springer, *Stabilizing the Debate Between Population-Centric and Enemy-Centric Counterinsurgency: Success Demands a Balanced Approach*, (Ft. Leavenworth, KS: U.S. Army Command and General Staff College, 2011), http://cgsc.contentdm.oclc.org/ cdm/singleitem/ collection/p4013coll2/id/2742 [accessed October 20, 2011], 1-6; and Valentina Taddeo, "U.S. Response to Terrorism: A Strategic Analysis of the Afghanistan Campaign," *Journal of Strategic Security*, Vol. 3, No. 2 (2010), http://scholarcommons.usf.edu/jss/ vol3/iss2/3 [accessed October 20, 2011], 27-38.

4. Miller, Greg, "U.S. officials believe al-Qaeda on brink of collapse," *The Washington Post* (July 21, 2011), http://www.washingtonpost.com/world/national-security/ al-qaeda-could-collapse-us-officials-say/2011/07/21/gIQAFu2pbI_story.html [accessed July 28, 2011].

5. John Brennan, interviewed by Judy Woodruff, *News Hour, PBS*, September 7, 2011, http://www.pbs.org/newshour/bb/politics/july-dec11/johnbrennan_09-07. html [accessed October 20, 2011]; John Brennan, "Strengthening our Security by Adhering to our Values and Laws," Office of the White House Press Secretary, Prepared remarks for the Harvard Law School Program on Law and Security, (September 16, 2011), http://www.whitehouse.gov/the-press-office/2011/09/16/ remarks-john-o-brennan-strengthening-our-security-adhering-our-values-an [accessed October 20, 2011].

6. *9/11 Commission Report: Final Report of the National Commission on Terrorist Attacks upon the United States* (New York: W. W. Norton, 2004), pp. 365–66.

7. The author uses "political defeat" in terms of the loss of political and national will for continued military actions against al Qaeda and its associated movements. For more information on al Qaeda's strategy and the caliphate, see Daveed Gartenstein-Ross, *Bin Laden's Legacy: Why We're Still Losing the War on Terror* (New York: John Wiley & Sons, 2011). For info on re-establishment of the caliphate, see ibid., pp. 22, 28-29, 42, 149, 155, 157. For specifics on AQ's strategy to economically defeat the U.S., see ibid., pp. 9-10, 14, 18, 21, 35-41.

8. Daveed Gartenstein-Ross, "Al-Qaeda on the Brink," *National Review Online*, (July 28, 2011), http://www.nationalreview.com/articles/272920/al-qaeda-brink-daveed-

gartenstein-ross [accessed July 29, 2011]. Additionally, see Gartenstein-Ross, *Bin Laden's Legacy*, for further details of his concepts presented in this article.

9. Ibid.

10. Henry Cuningham, "CIA Director Petraeus tell special ops meeting at Fort Bragg that people are the key to success," *Fayetteville Observer*, (November 3, 2011), http://fayobserver.com/articles/2011/ 11/03/ 1134605 [accessed November 6, 2011].

11. Andrew R. Molnar, William A Lybrand, Lorna Hahn, James L. Kirkman, and Peter B. Riddleberger, *Undergrounds in Insurgent, Revolutionary, and Resistance Warfare*, (Washington, DC: Special Operations Research Office, November 1963), http://handle.dtic.mil/100.2/AD436353 [accessed December 21, 2008], v.

12. Greg Grant, "Insurgency Chess Match: Allies Match Wits, Tactics with Ever-Changing Enemy in Iraq," *Defense News* (February 27, 2006), 6.

13. Associated Press Corps, "Iraqi Forces Weary of America's Troop Withdrawal," *Fox News* Web site (March 09, 2009), http://www.foxnews.com/story/0,2933,507544,00.html [accessed March 9, 2009].

14. The form, function, and logic construct used in this monograph is derived from Edward PW Hayward, *Planning Beyond Tactics: Towards a Military Application of the Philosophy of Design in the Formulation of Strategy*, (master's thesis, Fort Leavenworth, KS, 2008), http://usacac.army.mil/cac2/ SAMS/ HaywardMonograph-PhilosophyofDesign.pdf [accessed on March 2, 2009], 1. Hayward uses *"Form, Function and Logic* [author's emphasis] as a method of reducing the existential crisis between what we expect to happen…and what we actually experience." Hayward's use of form, function, and logic is derived from Gilles Deleuze and Felix Guattari, *A Thousand Plateaus; Capitalism and Schizophreni*, (Minneapolis: University of Minnesota Press, 1987); As Molnar, et. al., explain, "the emphasis in the study is on describing the functions and techniques of undergrounds." Molnar, et. al., 27.

15. Department of Defense, JP 3-24, *Counterinsurgency Operations*, (Washington, D.C.: U.S. Government Printing Office, 05 October 2009), GL-5; Counterguerrilla operations is defined as, "Operations and activities conducted by armed forces, paramilitary forces or nonmilitary agencies against guerrillas."

16. For example, author David C. Gompert noted in 2007, "[Counterinsurgency] operations could be improved by understanding and addressing the forms of networking that characterize the global insurgency. As mentioned earlier, recent works at RAND reveal the significance of jihadist 'nodes, hubs, and cores,' the first being fighters, terrorists, and other operatives; the second being the tier responsible for planning, financial operations, communications, material support, and providing direction to the nodes; and the third being the theoreticians and charismatic leaders. While a great deal of attention has been given to nodes and cores, this ongoing RAND work highlights the advantage of targeting *hubs*— the middle tiers that are critical to enabling nodes to turn ideological guidance of the cores into action." David C. Gompert, *Heads We Win: The Cognitive Side*

of *Counterinsurgency (COIN)*, (Santa Monica, CA: RAND Corporation, 2007), http://www.rand.org/pubs/occasional_papers/2007/RAND_OP168.pdf [accessed on March 4, 2009], 48-49; Also, The National Security Council noted, "The loss of a leader can degrade a [terrorist] group's cohesiveness and in some cases may trigger its collapse." National Security Council, *National Strategy for Combating Terrorism*, (Washington, D.C.: The White House, 2006), http://georgewbush-whitehouse.archives.gov/nsc/nss/2006/nss2006.pdf [accessed April 6, 2009], 12. For information on facilitators, see Anthony H. Cordesman, *Iraq's Sunni Insurgents: Looking Beyond Al Qa'ida*, (working draft, Washington, D.C.: Center for Strategic and International Studies, July 16, 2007), http://www.csis.org/ media/ csis/pubs/070716_sunni_insurgents.pdf [accessed on February 8, 2009], 2.

17. As author Linda Robinson notes, "Special Operations units…stepped up their already intense pace to target…Al-Qaeda's top three tiers of leaders, financiers, bomb-makers, and facilitators. The Al-Qaeda in Iraq (AQI) organization had proven its ability to regenerate almost as fast as the commandos captured or killed its leaders." Linda Robinson, *Tell Me How This Ends*, (New York, NY: Public Affairs, 2008), 56-7, 180.

18. Jeffrey White, *An Adaptive Insurgency: Confronting Adversary Networks in Iraq*, Policy Focus #58, (Washington, D.C.: The Washington Institute for Near East Policy, September 2006), http://www. washingtoninstitute.org/pubPDFs/Policy-Focus58.pdf [accessed March 23, 2009], 8.

19. Bob Woodward, *The War Within: A Secret White House History 2006-2008*, (New York, NY: Simon & Schuster, 2008), 59.

20. Ibid., 131. Other studies on targeting insurgent leaders have concluded that removing key leaders has limited long-term effect; for example, see Lisa Langdon, Alexander J. Sarapu, and Matthew Wells, "Targeting the leadership of terrorist and insurgent movements: Historical Lessons for Contemporary Policy Makers," *Journal of Public and International Affairs* 15, (Spring 2004): 73-76, http://www.princeton.edu/~jpia/pdf2004/Chapter%204.pdf [accessed on 23 March 2009]; Graham H. Turbiville, Jr., *Hunting Leadership Targets in Counterinsurgency and Counterterrorist Operations: Selected Perspectives and Experience*, Joint Special Operations University Report 07-6, (Hurlburt Field, FL: Joint Special Operations University, June 2007), http://jsoupublic.socom.mil/publications/jsou/ JSOU07-6-turbivilleHuntingLeadershipTargets_final.pdf [accessed on November 22, 2008], 1, 75-79; and Daniel Byman, *The Five Front War: The Better Way to Fight Global Jihad*, (Hoboken, NJ: John Wiley & Sons, 2008), 116-119, under "The Rewards and Costs of Targeted Killing."

21. CBS News, "U.S.: 2 of Al Qaeda's Top Leaders Killed in Iraq," *CBS News Web site* (April 19, 2010), http://www.cbsnews.com/stories/2010/04/19/world/main6410912.shtml [accessed February 10, 2010].

22. For example, RAND analysts Seth Jones and Martin Libicki explain, "A network is vulnerable, however, at its hubs. If enough hubs are destroyed, the network breaks down into isolated, noncommunicating islands of nodes. Hubs in a social network are vulnerable because most communications go through them. With good

intelligence, law-enforcement authorities should be able to identify and arrest these hubs." Seth G. Jones and Martin C. Libicki, *How Terrorist Groups End: Lessons from Countering al Qa'ida*, (Santa Monica, CA: RAND Corporation, 2008), http://www.rand.org/pubs/ monographs/2008/RAND_MG741-1.pdf [accessed March 23, 2009], 126; also see Byman, 94; under "Darwinian process."

23. Turbiville, 1-2, 9.

24. For example, noted terrorism expert Bruce Hoffman explains, "It is therefore possible that the insurgency in Iraq may indeed represent a new form of warfare for a new, networked century. It is too soon to determine whether this development, involving loose networks of combatants who come together for a discrete purpose only to quickly disperse upon its achievement, will prove to be a lasting or completely ephemeral characteristic of postmodern insurgency;" Bruce Hoffman, *Insurgency and Counterinsurgency in Iraq*, (Santa Monica, CA: RAND Corporation, 2004), http://www.rand.org/pubs/occasional_papers/ 2005/RAND_OP127. pdf [accessed on November 22, 2008], 18; Department of the Army, FM 3-24, *Counterinsurgency*, (Washington, D.C.: U.S. Government Printing Office, December 2006), http://usacac.army.mil/cac2/Repository/Materials/COIN-FM3-24.pdf [accessed January 15, 2009], 1-4.

25. For instance, see: Hoffman, *Insurgency*, 18; David Ronfeldt, "Al Qaeda and its affiliates: A global tribe waging segmental warfare?" *First Monday* 10, no. 3 (March 7, 2005), under "Abstract," http://firstmonday.org/issues/ issue10_3/ronfeldt/index. html [accessed March 4, 2009]; Mark Buchanan, *Nexus: Small Worlds and the Groundbreaking Science of Networks*, (New York, NY: W. W. Norton & Company, 2002), 21; John Arquilla and David Ronfeldt, *Networks and Netwars*, (Santa Monica, CA: RAND, 2001), http://www.rand.org/pubs/ monograph_reports/ MR1382/index.html [accessed on January 30, 2009], 6-16; Marc Sageman, *Leaderless Jihad: Terror Networks in the Twenty-First Century*, (Philadelphia, PA: University of Pennsylvania Press, 2008), 144; Marc Sageman, *Understanding Terror Networks*, (Philadelphia, PA: University of Pennsylvania Press, 2004), 137.

26. Buchanan, 21.

27. As Molnar, et. al., found, "Undergrounds have been the base of resistance and revolutionary movements throughout recorded history;" and that "it is clear that clandestine organizations are not the product of a particular political or religious ideology; cultural, ethnic, national, or geographic grouping of persons; structure or form of government; segment of society or social class; or stage of a society's economic or technological development. Also [sic] it is clear that undergrounds are not new nor unique to the contemporary world scene, although such an impression is easily created by the pressure of current problems. Underground movements directed toward changes in governing authority have appeared in societal life throughout recorded history." Molnar, et. al., 4, 23-26.

28. Roger Trinquier had a similar opinion based on his experiences in Algeria, explaining, "In seeking a solution, it is essential to realize that in *modern warfare* we are not up against just a few armed bands spread across a given territory, but rather against an *armed clandestine organization* whose essential role is to

impose its will upon the population. Victory will be obtained only through the complete destruction of that organization. This is the master concept that must guide us in our study of *modern warfare*." Roger Trinquier, *Modern Warfare: A French View of Counterinsurgency*, (London: Pall Mall Press, 1964), http://cgsc. leavenworth.army.mil/carl/resources/csi/trinquier/trinquier.asp [accessed January 15, 2009], 8-9.

29.   The Special Operations Research Office conducted the last major studies on undergrounds during Vietnam; see Molnar, et. al. The most notable U.S. effort to lethally counter insurgent undergrounds was the Phoenix Program in Vietnam. As author Charles Simpson explains "the concept was to identify and then capture or kill members of the Vietcong political or support personnel living undercover in disputed villages, or even in so-called pacified areas;" Charles M. Simpson III, *Inside the Green Berets: The First Thirty Years*, (Novato, CA: Presidio Press, 1983), 9; also see Dale Andrade, *Ashes to Ashes: The Phoenix Program and the Vietnam War*, (Lexington, MA: Lexington Books, 1990); Ken Tovo, "From the Ashes of the Phoenix: Lessons for Contemporary Counterinsurgency Operations," in *Strategic Challenges for Counterinsurgency and the Global War on Terrorism*, ed. Williamson Murray, (Carlisle, PA: Strategic Studies Institute, September 2006), http://www.strategicstudiesinstitute.army.mil/ pdffiles/PUB710. pdf [accessed March 5, 2009], 17-42; United States Military Assistance Command, *PHUNG HOANG Advisors Handbook*, (Vietnam: United States Military Assistance Command, November 20, 1970), http://www.virtual.vietnam.ttu.edu/ cgi-bin/starfetch.exe? cjGDEhjqEBDExu9fCcjH5b3O7 WlKcAYxLC5Cpx3X@ VJlyYEeHvEd5qSH NUIJ43IL6ur4w9KL5Vs J2XIamvRZF wD1ESf@ IDwdrC4x-8S60DoE/ 1370406001.pdf [accessed March 25, 2009].

30.   FM 3-24, see paragraph 1-70, page 1-13, and paragraph 1-95, page 1-17, organization and networks, respectively; Appendix B describes the use of social network analysis to map insurgent networks, but provides no other organizational analysis or information on clandestine cellular networks.

31.   JP 3-24, II-16 to II-20.

32.   Ibid., II-19; FM 3-24, 1-17; despite this statement, paragraph 1-87, page 1-16, states that "contemporary insurgencies often develop in urban environments, leveraging formal and informal networks for action. Understanding these networks is vital to defeating such insurgencies."

33.   For this monograph, Molnar's, et. al., definition of undergrounds is used: "Clandestine organizational elements of politico-military movements attempting to illegally weaken, modify, or replace the existing governing authority." Molnar, et. al., 13-15, 27. The author's definition of auxiliary is used and defined here as the active civilian support mechanism for the insurgency which conducts clandestine activities, such as logistics, intelligence, and operational support. For current examples of undergrounds, see David G. Fivecoat and Aaron T. Schwengler, "Revisiting *Modern Warfare*: Counterinsurgency in the Mada'in Qada," *Military Review* (November-December 2008), http://usacac.army.mil/CAC2/ MilitaryReview/Archives/English/MilitaryReview_20081231_art012.pdf [accessed

on March 2, 2009], 79; Fivecoat and Schwengler contrasted the Shi'a extremist militia organization with a clandestine Algerian cell structure from Trinquier's *Modern Warfare*, stating, "The Shi'a organization replicated the configuration Trinquier fought in Algeria in the late 1950s. This order of battle chart proved a valuable tool." Also see Shahid Afsar, Chris Samples, and Thomas Wood, "The Taliban: An Organizational Analysis," *Military Review* (May-June 2008), http://usacac.army.mil/CAC/milreview/ English/MayJun08/ SamplesEngMayJun08.pdf [accessed March 3, 2009], 65-67. The authors note that the Taliban is a networked organization, with, "Specialized departments at the Taliban's top and middle tiers," including specialized "departments" based on skills. At the lower levels, the Taliban operates more like a rural guerrilla army, but the authors describe these as "village cells" of "between 10 and 50 part-time fighters."

34. FM 3-24, 1-7, 1-13, 1-16, 1-17, and 1-23; Molnar, et. al., 13-15.

35. FM 3-24, 1-17; Department of the Army, FM 90-8, *Counterguerrilla Operations*, (Washington, D.C.: U.S. Government Printing Office, August 1986), 1-5. As FM 90-8 notes, "Counterguerrilla operations are geared to the active military elements of the insurgent movement only;" 1-5. Guerrilla warfare expert Virgil Ney shows this propensity of western counterinsurgency theories is to focus on the overt fighting forces of the insurgents has remained largely unchanged in the last fifty years, as he noted in 1961, "Western military writers have considered guerrilla warfare almost exclusively in purely military terms. They have been concerned primarily with the effectiveness of guerrilla tactics when employed against conventional armies;" Virgil Ney, *Guerrilla War: Principles and Practices*, (Washington, D.C.: Command Publications, 1961), 20; also, Trinquier identified this problem in Algeria, "[Operational commanders] have little interest in the less noble task, however essential, of subtle work with the population that enables guerrilla bands to survive despite local defeats the forces of order periodically inflict." Trinquier, 58; and Momboisse notes, "The importance of the underground is tremendous. Indeed without it the Revolution would not succeed. Unfortunately its importance is often ignored or greatly underrated…unquestionably due to the secrecy of its operation." Raymond M. Momboisse, *Blueprint of Revolution: The Rebel, The Party, The Technique of Revolt*, (Springfield, IL: Charles C Thomas, 1970), 62.

36. Frank Kitson, *Low Intensity Operations: Subversion, Insurgency, and Peacekeeping*, (St. Petersburg, FL: Hailer Publishing, no date), 68; Molnar, et. al., 14-15.

37. John J. McGrath, *The Other End of the Spear: The Tooth-to-Tail Ratio (T3R) in Modern Military Operations*, The Long War Series Occasional Paper 23, (Fort Leavenworth, KS: Combat Studies Institute Press, 2007), 2.

38. Ibid., 88.

39. Molnar, et. al., 13.

40. Figure 1 is based on data from Molnar, et. al., 14-15.

41. FM 3-24, 1-17; John J. McCuen, *The Art of Counter-Revolutionary War*, (St. Petersburg, FL: Hailer Publishing, 2005), 51; As guerrilla warfare expert Robert Taber

explains, "Analogically, the guerrilla fights the war of the flea, and his military enemy suffers the dog's disadvantage: too much to defend; too small, ubiquitous, and agile an enemy to come to grips with. If the war continues long enough—this is the theory—the dog succumbs to exhaustion and anemia without ever having found anything on which to close his jaws or to rake with his claws." Robert Taber, *The War of the Flea: A Study of Guerrilla Warfare Theory and Practice*, (New York, NY: Lyle Stuart, Inc., 1965), 27-28.

42.   Robinson, 11, 161-168; and Alireza Jafarzadeh, *The Iran Threat: President Ahmadinejad and the Coming Nuclear Crisis*, (New York, NY: Palgrave Mac-Millan, 2007), 81-87, 113-114, 116-119.

43.   FM 3-24, 1-17; Grant, 6; and Associated Press Corps.

44.   Department of the Army, Field Manual 3-05.201, *Special Forces Unconventional Warfare Operations*, (Washington, D.C.: U.S. Government Printing Office, April 30, 2003), 1-5. This version of the ARSOF UW manual is used instead of the current FM 3-05.201 due to the upgrade in classification of the current manual; see also, Department of the Army, Field Manual 31-20-3, *Foreign Internal Defense: Tactics, Techniques, and Procedures for Special Forces*, (Washington, D.C.: U.S. Government Printings Office, September 20, 1994), 1-7 to 1-10.

45.   Ibid.

46.   FM 3-05.201, 1-5.

47.   Ibid., 1-5 to 1-8.

48.   FM 3-24, 1-13 to 1-17.

49.   JP 3-24, II-9 to II-21.

50.   David Galula, *Counterinsurgency Warfare: Theory and Practice*, (St. Petersburg, FL: Hailer Publishing, 2005), 43-58; Kitson, 32-48, 128; McCuen, 30-37; Ney, 17-20, 44-46; Robert Thompson, *Defeating Communist Insurgency: Experiences from Malaya and Vietnam*, (London: Chatto&Windus, 1974), 28-42; and Trinquier, 10-15.

51.   Trinquier, 9.

52.   Ibid.

53.   Bard E. O'Neill, *Insurgency & Terrorism: From Revolution to Apocalypse*, 2nd ed., (Washington, DC: Potomac Books, 2005), Chapter 6; Bruce Hoffman, "Combating Al Qaeda and the Militant Islamic Threat," testimony presented to the House Armed Service Committee, Subcommittee on Terrorism, Unconventional Threats and Capabilities, February 16, 2009, (Santa Monica, CA: RAND Corporation, 2006), http://www.rand.org/ pubs/testimonies/2006/ RAND_CT255.pdf [accessed January 15, 2009], 3-6; John Arquilla, "It Takes a Network: On Countering Terrorism While Reforming the Military," testimony before the House Armed Service Subcommittee on Terrorism, Unconventional Threats and Capabilities, (September 18, 2008), http://armedservices.house.gov/pdfs/TUTC091808/ Arquilla_Testimony091808.pdf [accessed November 22, 2008], 1.

54.   O'Neill, 134-135.

55.   Gompert, 48-49; Ori Brafman and Rod A. Beckstrom, *The Starfish and the Spider: The Unstoppable Power of Leaderless Organizations*, (New York, NY: Penguin Group, 2006), 5; Also, Sageman explains, "Where a small-world network is vulnerable to targeted attack is at its hubs. If enough hubs are destroyed, the network breaks down into isolated, noncommunicating islands of nodes." Sageman, *Understanding*, 140. Arquilla noted in his congressional testimony that the U.S. is in what he calls, "an 'organizational race' to build networks [and]....The terrorists remain on their feet and fighting, in large part because their nimble, networked structures have been given the opportunity to keep developing, their hallmarks being the decentralization of authority, the proliferation of small cells throughout the world, and an abundance of lateral links – many in cyberspace – among and between their many nodes." Arquilla, 1. Authors Michele Zanini and Sean Edwards explain, "What has been emerging in the business world is now becoming apparent in the organizational structures of the newer and more active terrorist groups, which appear to be adopting decentralized, flexible network structures. The rise of the networked arrangements in terrorist organization is part of a wider move away from the formally organized...groups." Michele Zanini and Sean J.A. Edwards, "The Networking of Terror in the Information Age," in *Networks and Netwars*, ed. John Arquilla and David Ronfeldt, (Santa Monica, CA: RAND, 2001), http://www.rand.org/pubs/ monograph_reports/MR1382/index.html [accessed January 30, 2009], 32. Also, Sageman applies information age theories in his book, *Understanding Terror Network*, explaining, "In more formal language, growth of this [terrorist] network was not a random process but one of preferential attachment, meaning that the probability that a new node will connect to any given node is *proportional to the number of its existing links* [author's emphasis-further violating the principles of clandestine arts]....a small-world network resists fragmentation because of its dense interconnectedness... Hubs in social networks are vulnerable...law enforcement authorities should be able to identify and arrest these human hubs. This strategy has already shown considerable success [author's emphasis]." Sageman, *Understanding*, 139-141.

As theorists Peter Holme, et. al., note, "None of the network models shows a behavior very similar to the real-world networks....This clearly suggests that there are other structures contributing to the network behavior during vertex attack, and conclusions from model networks should be cautiously generalized to real-world situations." Petter Holme, Boem Jun Kim, Chang No Yoon, and Seung Kee Han, "Attack vulnerability of complex networks," *Physical Review* E 65 (2002): 12, http://nlsc.ustc.edu.cn/ BJKim/PAPER/ PhysRevE_65_056109%20Attack%20vulnerability%20of%20complex%20networks.pdf [accessed January 30, 2009]. Note theorist Stephen Borgatti focused on identifying key players within terrorist networks for attack with three goals,"(a) identifying nodes whose deletion would maximally fragment the network, (b) identifying nodes that, based on structural position alone, are potentially 'in the know', [sic] and (c) identifying nodes that are in a position to influence others." Stephen P. Borgatti, "Identifying Sets of Structurally Key Players," (lecture, Carnegie Mellon University Center for Computational Analysis of Social and Organizational Systems (CASOS), June 21, 2002), http://www.casos.cs.cmu.edu/publications/papers/ CASOSConf_2002_Day1.pdf [accessed November 22, 2008], 69; and Jonathan David Farley, "Breaking Al Qaeda Cells: A Mathematical Analysis of Counterterrorism Operations (A Guide for Risk Assessment and Decision Making)," *Studies in Conflict & Terrorism* 26, no. 26 (June 2003), 409. Farley attempts to develop a technique for determining the degree that a terrorist cell functions, to identify "when a battle against Al Qaeda has been won." Although interesting, it shows the confusion of terms between cells and networks. He also falsely believes that his theory can successfully neutralize a cell or network by cutting the leadership off from the cell members.

For an examples of theorists that are beginning to identify weaknesses in network attack models, see: renowned social network theorist, Kathleen Carley, who notes, "Many are stepping forward suggesting that to understand [covert] networks we just need to 'connect the dots' and then isolate 'key actors…in the network;" Carley further explains that attacking key actors "does not contend with the most pressing problem – the underlying network is dynamic. Just because you isolate a key actor…today…does not mean that the network will be destabilized and unable to respond." see Kathleen M. Carley, *Estimating Vulnerabilities in Large Covert Networks*, (Pittsburgh, PA: Carnegie Mellon University, Institute for Software Research International, June 2004), http://www.dtic.mil/cgi-bin/ GetTRDoc?AD=ADA466095& Location=U2&doc=GetTRDoc.pdf [accessed November 22, 2008], 2; and see Maksim Tsvetovat and Kathleen M. Carley, "Bouncing Back: Recovery Mechanisms of Covert Networks," (paper presented at the *NAACSOS Conference 2003*, Day 3, Pittsburgh, PA, June 2003), http:// www. casos.cs.cmu.edu/ publications/papers/tsvetovat_2003_ bouncingback.pdf [accessed November 22, 2008], ii.

56.   Department of Defense, Joint Publication 1-02, *Department of Defense Diction- ary of Military and Associated Terms*, (Washington, D.C.: Government Printing Office, November 8, 2010, amended September 15, 2011), http://www.dtic.mil/ doctrine/new_pubs/jp1_02.pdf [accessed October 20, 2011], 53. As JP 1-02 notes, "A clandestine operation differs from a covert operation in that emphasis is placed on concealment of the operation rather than on concealment of the identity of the sponsor."

57.   Department of the Army, Pamphlet No. 550-104, *Human Factors Considerations of Undergrounds in Insurgencies*, (Washington, DC: Headquarters, Depart- ment of the Army, September 1966), http://cgsc.cdmhost.com/cgi-bin/showfile. exe?CISOROOT=/p4013coll9&CISOPTR=85 [accessed November 22, 2008], 101.

58.   Fred Burton defines tradecraft as "the set of skills needed to conduct clandestine activities in a hostile environment without discovery." Fred Burton, "Beware of 'Kramer': Tradecraft and the New Jihadists," *STRATFOR* (January 19, 2006), http://www.stratfor.com/beware_kramer_tradecraft_and _new_jihadists [accessed November 16, 2008], under title.

59.   The literature on undergrounds and clandestine operations varies. The most acces- sible for the Western reader are numerous accounts of clandestine operations from

American and British World War II (WWII) veterans that served, in the British Special Operations Executive (SOE), the American Office of Strategic Services (OSS)—the precursor to the Central Intelligence Agency (CIA), including M. R. D. Foot, *SOE: The Special Operations Executive 1940-1946*, (n.p.: University Publications of America, Inc., 1986); Will Irwin, *The Jedburghs: The Secret History of the Allied Special Forces, France 1944*, (New York, NY: Public Affairs, 2005); and Russell Miller, *Behind The Lines: The Oral History of Special Operations in World War II*, (New York, NY: New American Library, 2002). Author Sherri Greene Ottis provides an outstanding history of the escape and evasion lines in WWII occupied France, including the clandestine techniques, cellular networks, and German counternetwork operations, in *Silent Heroes: Downed Airmen and the French Underground*, (Lexington, KY: The University Press of Kentucky, 2001).

For informative works on undergrounds, including two by the Special Operations Research Office, see: DA PAM 550-104; Raymond M. Momboisse, *Blueprint of Revolution: The Rebel, The Party, The Technique of Revolt*, (Springfield, IL: Charles C Thomas, 1970); H. von Dach Bern, *Total Resistance: Swiss Army Guide to Guerrilla Warfare and Underground Operations*, ed. R. K. Brown, (Boulder, CO: Panther Publications, Inc., 1965); and Trinquier.

Espionage related works that provide extensive background on clandestine techniques include: Richard M. Bennett, *Espionage: Spies and Secret*, (London: Virgin Books Ltd, 2003); Alexander Orlov, *Handbook of Intelligence and Guerrilla Warfare*, (Ann Arbor, MI: The University of Michigan Press, 1965); I.E. Prikhodko, *Characteristics of Agent Communications and of Agent Handling in the United States of America*, (San Francisco, CA: Interservice Publishing Company, Inc., 1981); Roy Godson, *Dirty Tricks or Trump Cards: U.S. Covert Action & Counterintelligence*, (New Brunswick, NJ: Transaction Publishers, 2004); Allen W. Dulles, *The Craft of Intelligence: America's Legendary Spy Master on the Fundamentals of Intelligence Gathering for a Free World*, (Guilford, CT: The Lyons Press, 2006); and Lindsay Moran, *Blowing My Cover: My life as a CIA Spy*, (New York, NY: Penguin Group, 2005).

60. See Mark Owen, *A Discussion of Covert Channels and Steganography*, (n.p.: SANS Institute, March 19, 2002), http://www.sans.org/reading_room/whitepapers/covert/a_discussion_of_ covert_channels_and_steganography_678?show=678.php&cat=covert [accessed March 5, 2009], 1; Patrick Di Justo, "How Al-Qaida Site Was Hijacked." WIRED, (August 10, 2002), http://www.wired.com/culture/lifestyle/news/2002/08/54455 [accessed March 7, 2009]; and Jim Wingate, *The Perfect Deaddrop: The Use of Cyberspace for Covert Communications*, (West Virginia: Steganography Analysis and Research Center (SARC), n.d.), http://www.infosec-technologies.com/steganograph.pdf [accessed January 31, 2009], 2. Also a history of U.S. spy Robert Hanssen notes, "Hanssen and his Russian intelligence handlers used simple, time-honored tradecraft to communicate with each other.... Although Hanssen had substantial communications with the KGB about using sophisticated computer techniques for communications, they used no sophisticated communications devices or modern technology but relied on the U.S. postal service, the telephone, and signal sites and deaddrops." *A Counterintelligence*

Reader. Edited by Frank J. Rafalko. http://www.fas.org/ irp/ops/ ci/docs/index. html [accessed March 25, 2009], 102.

61.   As defined on *Merriam-Webster Online Dictionary*, http://www.merriam-webster. com/ dictionary/form%5B1%5D [accessed February 16, 2009].

62.   DA PAM 550-104, 19.

63.   Orlov, 152.

64.   FM 3-05.130, 4-6 to 4-8; FM 3-24, 1-11 and 1-12. FM 3-24 dropped this construct and opted for broader five-component model consisting of movement leaders, combatants, political cadre, auxiliaries, and the mass base; JP 3-24, II-16 to II-20. JP 3-24 returns to the ARSOF model, with Guerrillas, Auxiliary, and Underground as "elements of an insurgency," but also adds in Strategic Leaders. JP3-24 further delineates "organization," with elements (explained above) and components which consist of the political wing, shadow government, supporting parties, military wing, and the mass base; The ARSOF three-component model is focused on the active supporters to the insurgency. Largely beyond the scope of this monograph, there is a fourth component, the mass support base, but these are generally the passive elements that support the insurgency or are neutral. This components will only be discussed here as a pool of possible recruits for the growth of the movement or replacement for movement members that are killed or captured, thus moving from passive support to active support and into one of the three components. In the three-component model, the first component to develop in an insurgency is the underground.

65.   DA PAM 550-104, 1; FM 3-05.201, 3-31 to 3-34; and Molnar, et. al., 23-29.

66.   FM 3-05.201, 3-33 to 3-34.

67.   Ibid., 3-24 to 3-30; and Molnar, et. al., 28.

68.   FM 3-05.201, 3-24 to 3-30.

69.   Ibid., 1-1, 3-18 to 3-24.

70.   Ibid.

71.   FM 3-24, 1-7.

72.   Roger Roy observes, "The brothers [suspected Afghan insurgents] shook hands with the Americans, and the soldiers filed out of the compound empty-handed, facing the tough truth about their job here: The foolish and the foolhardy among the insurgents—the low-hanging fruit on the terrorist tree—have, like the apples in [one of the brother's] orchard, already been plucked. Those who have survived this long won't be easy to catch." Roger Roy, "Tracking down Afghan insurgents like a "chess game" for U.S. troops," *The Seattle Times*, November 28, 2005, under "Fruitless Search," http://seattletimes.nwsource. com/cgi-bin/PrintStory. pl?document_id=2002650678& zsection_id= 2002107549&slug=afghanenemy28& date=20051128 [accessed March 19, 2009].

73.   FM 3-05.201, 1-7 to 1-8. Mao's three phases are the strategic defensive, the strategic stalemate, and the strategic counteroffensive; FM 3-24, 1-6; other theorists, such

as John McCuen uses a four phased model: organization, terrorism, guerrilla warfare, and mobile warfare, giving terrorism its own phase; McCuen, 40.

74. Momboisse, Chapters 17-20.

75. Ibid., Chapters 21 and 22.

76. FM 3-05.201, 1-8. War-of-movement phase is the final phase when an insurgency transitions from guerrilla warfare to conventional warfare.

77. See Valdis E. Krebs, "Uncloaking Terrorist Networks," *First Monday*, vol. 7, no. 4 (April 1, 2002), http://firstmonday.org/htbin/cgiwrap/bin/ojs/index.php/fm/article/view/941/863 [accessed November 22, 2008].

78. DA PAM 550-104, 2; McCuen, 40. McCuen also uses a similar sub-phase model as well for undergrounds based on a French model referred to as "Trotsky's Five Phases of Revolution;" 42.

79. DA PAM 550-104, 2; and Momboisse, Chapter 4.

80. DA PAM 550-104, 2; and Momboisse, 157, 220, 223-233, 238, 247, 262.

81. DA PAM 550-104, 2-3.

82. Ibid., 3.

83. For information on oil spot theory see Robert J. Ward, "Oil Spot: Spreading Security to Counter Insurgency," *Special Warfare* 20, no.2 (March-April 2007): 8-17. http://www.soc.mil/swcs/swmag/ 07Mar.pdf [accessed March 2, 2009]; "In 1954 General Challe introduced the 'spot-of-oil' strategy in an effort to pacify the Algerians." Molnar, et. al., 169.

84. Author's figure.

85. DA PAM 550-104, 2, 19-26.

86. Ibid., 20-23; see Figure 2 on page 22.

87. Ibid., 20-21.

88. Based on functional cell figures 1-3, DA PAM 550-104, 21-23.

89. Ibid., 20-26.

90. Ibid., 24-25.

91. Based on Figures 4-5, DA PAM 550-104, 25-26.

92. A contemporary example of cell-in-series is an improvised explosive device (IED) branch or sub-network, in which the branch leader coordinates the actions of his different cells. The individual cells have no knowledge of the role or identity of the other cells within series. Thus, the branch leader directs his intelligence cell to identify a specific type of security forces vehicle to target and to develop its operational pattern. Another cell may build the appropriate IED, and place it in a cache. Simultaneously the cell's intelligence collector determines the most likely route that vehicle takes and builds the vehicles pattern of movement to determine the best time and location to interdict the target. Once the location for the IED ambush has been identified, the leader directs the support cell to dig the hole for the IED. Once dug, the leader directs another cell, to recover the IED from the

cache, and emplace the device. Lastly, a triggerman, from the operations cell, is provided with the means to detonate the device and the target description of the type of security force vehicle the IED was built to destroy, and conducts the operation. If he films the event, then he drops off the film at a drop-off point, and notifies the cell leader that the operation is complete. The cell leader directs the media cell to pick up the film from the drop-off site, and put it on the Internet after editing it. See Grant, 6.

93. Grant, 6.

94. Based on author's experience in Iraq. Insurgent leaders routinely moved between safe houses or safe locations based on the pressure from counterinsurgency forces, moving every few days to every few hours. Also see Bern, 110; Foot, 128.

95. Albert-László Barabási, *Linked: How Everything is Connected to Everything Else and What It Means for Business, Science, and Everyday Life*, (New York, NY: Penguin Group, 2003), 16-17, 77-78; As complexity theorists Simon Reay Atkinson and James Moffat explain: "Random Networks form through individuals meeting up by accident rather than by design;"and Simon Reay Atkinson and James Moffat, *The Agile Organization: From Linear Networks to Complex Effects and Agility*, (Washington, D. C.: DoD Command and Control Research Program, July 2005), http://www.dodccrp.org/files/ Atkinson_Agile.pdf [accessed January 12, 2009]. 97; Atkinson and James explain further, that small-world networks are defined by a low path length, or the "number of intermediate acquaintances that link one person to the other." 46; And finally, they explain that scale-free network links are based not on randomness, but based on an observation of the "richness of connection," or the number of links a node has, which increases the "richness of connection" of the node, which in turn causes these rich nodes to be connected to by random nodes due to "preferential attachment;" 47.

96. Figure based on the author's experiences and network diagrams from the following: Grant, 6; Kitson, 68,128; Molnar, et. al., 54, 204, 273, 300, and 319; DA PAM 550-104, 21-26; Trinquier, 11; Malcolm W. Nance, *Terrorist Recognition Handbook: Practitioner's Manual for Predicting and Identifying Terrorist Activities*, 2nd ed., (Boca Raton, FL: CRC Press, Taylor & Francis Group, 2008), 75-79; Thompson, 31; Bern, 86-89; Fivecoat and Schwengler, 79; Afsar, Samples, and Wood, 65-67. The authors note that the Taliban is a networked organization, with, "Specialized departments at the Taliban's top and middle tiers," including specialized "departments" based on skills. At the lower levels, the Taliban operates more like a rural guerrilla army, but the authors describe these as "village cells" of "between 10 and 50 part-time fighters."

97. Grant, 6.

98. Barabási, 17-18; Yaneer Bar-Yam, *Making Things Work: Solving Complex Problems in a Complex World*, (Cambridge, MA: NESCI Knowledge Press, 2004), 98-99; Sageman, Leaderless, vii, 69, 144; Brafman and Beckstrom, 5. Brafman and Beckstrom explain, "This book is about what happens when there's no one in charge. It's about what happens when there's no hierarchy."

99. Ibid.; However, even though many theorist consider al-Qaeda to have "leaderless" affiliates, the al-Qaeda Training Manual makes it clear that there is to be a leader even if there are only three members, "'When they assemble, it is necessary to [have] a leader. Allah's prophet – God bless and keep him – even said, 'If three [people] come together let them pick a leader.'" *The Al Qaeda Manual*, trans.by the Manchester (England) Metropolitan Police, (no other publication data). http://www.au.af.mil/au/ awc/ awcgate/terrorism/alqaida_manual/ manualpart1_1.pdf [accessed November 24, 2008], BM-12.

100. Jeffrey, 5, 8.

101. See Simson L. Garfinkel, "Leaderless resistance today," *First Monday*, vol. 8, no. 3 (March 2003): under "An introduction to leaderless resistance," http://firstmonday.org/issues/issue8_3/garfinkel/ index.html [accessed January 8, 2009]. As Garfinkel highlights, "Leaderless Resistance...has been used by white supremacists, anti-abortion and environmental activists, and animal rights groups. I argue that, despite the problems inherent in Leaderless Resistance, this structure is well-suited to many ideologies. Furthermore, many problems inherent in classic Leaderless Resistance can be overcome through modern communications technology. *This is not to say that Leaderless Resistance is an effective strategy for achieving a movement's stated aims. To the contrary, the adoption of Leaderless Resistance by a movement should be regarded as an admission of failure.* [author's emphasis] In many ways, Leaderless Resistance is a last-ditch effort to keep a struggle alive in the face of an overwhelming opposition."

102. As 550-104 notes, "There is a great deal of local autonomy with respect to specific actions which require adjustment to local conditions. Tactical decisions are usually made independently by lower-echelon leaders in decentralized commands.... There are two factors that dictate this practice. The first is that the local units probably know the situation better than the central command, and the second is that the lower echelons are probably better prepared to makes decisions with respect to implementation and time." Also see Grant, 6; "Each network concentrates its operations in a small geographic area such as a neighborhood or village, allowing each to focus on a specific American unit." DA PAM 550-104, 26-27.

103. DA PAM 550-104, 2, 20; Prikhodko, 18-19; and Bennett, *Espionage*, 69.

104. As defined on *Merriam-Webster Online Dictionary*, http://www.merriam-webster.com/ dictionary/compartmentalization [accessed February 16, 2009].

105. DA PAM 550-104, 2.

106. Trinquier, 39.

107. Prikhodko, 18-19; DA PAM 550-104, 2, 20; and Bennett, *Espionage*, 69.

108. DA PAM 550-104, 20; Al Qaeda, BM-52-BM 55; as Grant notes, "Keeping his hands clean, [the network leader] avoids direct involvement in attacks by assigning operations and their planning to his lieutenants." Grant, 6; Bymann quotes a senior al-Qaeda leader stating, "'When four people know the details of an operation, it is dangerous; when two people know, it is good; when just one person knows, it is better.'" Byman,109; also, as the al-Qaeda training manual explains,

"Keeping Secrets and Concealing Information," it states, "[This secrecy should be used] even with the closest people, for deceiving the enemies is not easy...."Seek Allah's help in doing your affairs in secrecy." Al Qaeda, BM-16.

109.   DA PAM 550-104, 2, 20.

110.   Ottis provides a good example of effective compartmentalization from evasion line networks in WWII, "Each escape line worker was one small link in a very big chain....While the workers concentrated on doing their jobs to the best of their ability, they did so without knowledge of the results of their efforts.....[One escape line worker] still [in 2001] does not know the details surrounding his involvement with the escape lines [in WWII]. His father maintained communications with the escape organization, and [the worker] simply followed his father's directions, escorting the evaders when and where he was told." Ottis, 68.

111.   Barnes, 44; Barnes' article captures the risk of direct contact between cell members, as the entire cell in this story is captured based on the questioning of individual members, thus revealing the names of the other members of the cell, which eventually leads to their arrest.

112.   Figure based on author's experience. Figure shows results of intelligence-driven counternetwork operations against both strong and weak clandestine cellular networks.

113.   DA PAM 550-104, 207-208; also see Ottis, 20; Ottis provides an example of inadvertently negating the compartmentalization between networks from World War II evasion line in Europe, where it was discovered by the allies that two different escape lines were using the same rendezvous points without either network knowing. The allies were able to contact the two networks to deconflict. However, had the location been compromised to German security forces do to clandestine failures of one network, the other would have likely been discovered as well.

114.   Cascading failure normally refer to "overload failures" of complex non-human networks, but is used here in the sense of a counterinsurgent using intelligence driven operations, to "roll-up" targets in quick succession. For more information on cascading failures of non-human networks, see Adilson E. Motter and Ying-Cheng Lai, "Cascade-based attacks on complex networks," *Physical Review* E 66, (December 20, 2002): 1-4, http://chaos1.la.asu.edu/~yclai/papers/PRE_02_ML_3.pdf [accessed March 4, 2002. Also see Ottis, 96; Ottis provides a perfect example of a cascading failure due to poor compartmentalization, where a captured network leader provided the Germans over one hundred names of evasion line members, leading to the arrest of most.

115.   Author's figure. The figure portrays intelligence-driven operations against both strong and weak clandestine cellular networks. Intelligence driven operations are frustrated when the counterinsurgents encounter the compartmentalization. Despite the significant success against the weak network, the operations still fail to decisively disrupt or defeat the network. Without knowledge of the true size of the network, the counterinsurgents are unable to effectively assess success or failure.

116. Ibid; portrays the results of the intelligence driven raid.

117. This monograph uses the following definition of unconventional warfare: "operations by a state or non-state actor to support an insurgency or resistance aimed at the overthrow of a government [recognized or unrecognized by the international community, i.e. the Taliban] or an occupying power;" from D. Jones, *Ending the Debate: Unconventional Warfare, Foreign Internal Defense, and Why Words Matter,* (master's thesis, Fort Leavenworth, 2006), http://cgsc.cdmhost.com/cgi-bin/showfile.exe?CISOROOT=/ p4013coll2& CISOPTR=554&filename=555. pdf [accessed December 21, 2008], 165-166. For example, the al Qaeda Training Manual states, "The main mission for which the Military Organization is responsible is: The overthrow of the godless regimes and their replacement with an Islamic regime." *Al Qaeda Manual*, BM-12.

118. See Jafarzadeh, 81-87; and Robinson, 107, 164,166-167, 342; White, 4; and Anthony H. Cordesman, *Iran's Revolutionary Guards, the Al Quds Force, and Other Intelligence and Paramilitary Forces,* (rough working draft, Washington, D.C.: Center for Strategic and International Studies, July 16, 2007), http://www.csis.org/media/csis/pubs/070816_cordesman_report.pdf [accessed February 8, 2009].

119. Jones, 165-166.

120. Molnar, et. al., 14-15.

121. David C. Gompert, "U.S. Should Take Advantage of Improved Security in Iraq to Withdraw" *San Francisco Chronicle* (December 2, 2007). http://www.rand.org/commentary/2007/12/02/SFC.html [accessed November 10, 2008].

122. David Birch, *The King's Chessboard*, (New York, NY: Puffin Books, July 1993).

123. Ibid.

124. Birch. There are 64 squares on a chessboard and the exponential growth pattern is 1, 2, 4, 8, 16, 32, 64, 128, 256, 512, 1024, 2048, 4096, 8192, 16384, 32768, 65536, 131072, 262144, 524288, 1048576, 2097152, 4194304, 8388608, 16777216, 33554432, 67108864, 134217728, 268435456, 536870912, 1073741824, 2147483648, with the last number being to 32 squares from "The King's Chessboard Solution," http://educ.queensu.ca/~fmc/march2003/KingsChessboardSoln.html [accessed March 5, 2009].

125. As one insurgent explained to author Zaki Chehab, "'We started this national front with ten people. We then opened it up to more people, and with the help of the faithful and those who believe in our cause, we have expanded to the extent that we have bases or cells all over Iraq.'" Zaki Chehab, *Inside the Resistance: The Iraqi Insurgency and the Future of the Middle East,* (New York, NY: Nation Books, 2005). Also, as Grant notes, "U.S. military officers described one such insurgent network, which calls itself the Islamic Patriotism Movement. Numbering about 55 fighters and led by a former Iraqi intelligence officer named Abu Omar, the network is loosely affiliated with the large Sunni insurgent group known as the Secret Islamic Army that operates throughout Iraq." Grant, 6.

126. The author's open network construct is adapted from open and closed systems as described by the father of General Systems Theory, L. von Bertalanffy. Bertalanffy

described a closed system, adapted in this case to networks, as "considered to be isolated from their environment." Using the same construct, an open network, based on the adaptation of system to network, is not isolated from their environment due to the requirement for purposeful growth; L. von Bertalanffy, *General Systems Theory*, 5th ed., (England: Penguin University Press, 1975), 38, 149, quoted in Shimon Naveh, *In Pursuit of Military Excellence: the Evolution of Operational Theory*, (Portland, OR: Frank Cass Publishers, 2000), 5.

127.   Krebs.

128.   For example, see Barabási, 222-224; Borgatti, 1; and Matthew J. Dombroski and Kathleen Carley, "NETEST: Estimating a Terrorist Network's Structure," (lecture, Carnegie Mellon University Center for Computational Analysis of Social and Organizational Systems (CASOS), June 21, 2002), http://www.casos.cs.cmu.edu/publications/ papers/CASOSConf_2002_Day1.pdf [accessed November 22, 2008],13-16.

129.   As defined on *MSN Encarta Online Dictionary*, http://encarta.msn.com/dictionary_ 1861613874/function.html [accessed February 25, 2009].

130.   DA PAM 550-104, 6.

131.   Hoffman, Insurgency, 17-18.

132.   Ibid.

133.   White, 4-5; author's experience with members of the "Sons of Iraq," April 2007-November 2007.

134.   For example, see Barnes, 44. Barnes captures the effectiveness of cut-outs and compartmentalization when the captured cell leader explains during questioning, "'Someone met me in Halibeah and gave me the [improvised explosive devices]'.... He professes not to know names;" also see Robinson, 180. As Robinson highlights, "Doing so required a tip on one suspect's current location to permit 'time-sensitive targeting,' and his capture would lead to the next, and the next. On one single night, twenty-seven Al-Qaeda targets were successfully captured."

135.   Robinson, 180. As Robinson explains, "The Al-Qaeda in Iraq (AQI) organization had proven its ability to regenerate almost as fast as the commandos captured or killed its leaders."

136.   Non-attribution discussion with a former infantry battalion commander on his unit's operations against cells in Iraq, February 2006, Ft. Leavenworth, Kansas.

137.   Jeffrey, 1, 4-5, 8.

138.   Author's diagram.

139.   See personal and impersonal communications, Prikhodko, 4, 19.

140.   Prikhodko, 19.

141.   Ibid.

142.   DA PAM 550-104, 102.

143.   Active and passive measures are the author's construct.

144.   Prikhodko, 19; and DA PAM 550-104, 20, 104.

145. David Tucker and Christopher J. Lamb, *United States Special Operations Forces*, (New York, NY: Columbia University Press, 2007), 208-209.

146. DA PAM 550-104, 103; Orlov, 148-150; and Prikhodko, 18. Prikhodko places couriers within the category of personal communications, yet refers to couriers as a cutout, explaining "A 'cut-out' is an agent or subordinate officer used as an intermediary between the officer and the agent, to make surveillance more difficult." The author chose to keep courier as a method of impersonal communications due to the lack of interaction between the leader and subordinate. Also see Jones and Libicki, 129; Jones and Libicki highlight that, "[al Qa'ida] adopted a four-tiered courier system to communicate among key members of the group and *minimize detectability* [emphasis added]. Many al Qa'ida leaders have become more cautious in using cell phones, satellite phones, email, and other forms of communication that foreign intelligence services can easily track."

147. Ottis, 78-79.

148. Bern, 115; Orlov, 148-150; and DA PAM 550-104, 59.

149. For translation of the letter, see Jumada al-Thani, trans., "Letter from al-Zawahiri to al-Zarqawi," *GlobalSecurity.org*, (July 9, 2005), http://www.globalsecurity.org/security/library/report/2005/ zawahiri-zarqawi-letter_9jul2005.htm [accessed January 19, 2009].

150. Trinquier, 13; Prikhodko, 20-21; Orlov, 150-151; Miller, 15; and DA PAM 550-104, 20-22, 33, 60.

151. Orlov, 152; and DA PAM 550-104, 20-22, 33.

152. Trinquier, 13.

153. Orlov, 152-153.

154. Ibid., 153.

155. Prikhodko, 19; and Miller, 71.

156. DA PAM 550-104, 20-22, 104.

157. Ibid.

158. Prikhodko, 23; and DA PAM 550-104, 231. 550-104 refers to this method as the "double-language technique" in which a form of media is used, but "contain messages and instructions coded in key words and phrases."

159. 159 Prikhodko, 25-27.

160. 160 Foot, 99.

161. SPOOK86 explains, "You may recall that some of Al Qaida's earliest tapes depicted bin Laden and his deputy in outdoor settings (the nature hike, as some intel wags called it). The pastoral scenes ended when it was revealed that the CIA had hired geologists familiar with the rock formations of Afghanistan and Pakistan. Examining the rocks provided potential clues to the whereabouts of bin Laden and Zawahiri. More recent videos showed Zawahiri in front of a cloth or canvas backdrop. But even that "neutral" backdrop can reveal information that may lead analysts to a particular region where that material is commonly used."

SPOOK86 [pseud.], "The Tape Zawahiri Had to Release," *In From the Cold*, formerspook.blogspot, entry posted January 31, 2006, http://formerspook.blogspot. com/2006/01/tape-zawahiri-had-to-release.html [accessed January 24, 2009].

162. Grant, 6.

163. Tucker and Lamb, 208-209; Byman, 96, 110; and Sageman, *Understanding*, 158-167.

164. Grant, 6.

165. See Wingate, 2; and Byman, 90.

166. Byman, 85, 107.

167. See Di Justo.

168. As the al Qaeda training manual states, "It is well known that in undercover operations, communication is the mainstay of the movement for rapid accomplishment. However, it is a double-edged sword: It can be to our advantage if we use it well and it can be a knife dug into our back if we do not consider and take the necessary security measures." *Al Qaeda Manual*, BM-85 to BM-90.

169. Prikhodko, 4.

170. "Information and orders are passed during face-to-face meetings in mosques, where U.S. troops rarely go." Grant, 6.

171. Prikhodko, 4.

172. Prikhodko, 4-13; Bern, 112-114; and Orlov, 110-125.

173. Bern, 112; and DA PAM 550-104, 243-244.

174. DA PAM 550-104, 243-244. Mechanical techniques include "wiretaps or concealed microphones."

175. See *Al Qaeda Manual*, BM-85 to BM-90; this entire section is on how to conduct and defeat surveillance.

176. Orlov, 110-125; and DA PAM 550-104, 104.

177. DA PAM 550-104, 243-244.

178. Mark Bowden, "The Ploy," *The Atlantic* (May 2008): 4, http://www.theatlantic. com/doc/ 200705/tracking-zarqawi [accessed November 28, 2008]. As explained by a Abu Hayder, a detainee and a high-level associate of Zarqawi, "He explained that Rahman, a figure well-known to the Task Force, met regularly with Zarqawi. He said that whenever they met, Rahman observed a security ritual that involved changing cars a number of times. Only when he got into a small blue car, Abu Haydr said, would he be taken directly to Zarqawi.

179. DA PAM 550-104, 101.

180. Grant, 6.

181. DA PAM 550-104, 103-107. 550-104 provides an example of countering inspection by security forces of hidden cargo, "An illegal cargo was covered with a tarpaulin and a layer of fresh manure. The police disliked searching such a load too closely and the cargo got through police inspection without being stopped;" 106.

182. Prikhodko, 14; former Central Intelligence Agency case officer, Lindsay Moran refers to this exact same technique as a "'surveillance detection route." Moran, Lindsay, *Blowing My Cover: My life as a CIA Spy*, (New York, NY: Penguin Group, 2005), 120.

183. Prikhodko, 14.

184. Ibid.

185. Orlov, 112-115, 156-157; and Clarence Ashley, *CIA Spy Master*, (Gretna, LA: Pelican Publishing Company, Inc., 2004), 231.

186. Ottis, 92; Miller, 71-72; *Al Qaeda Manual*, BM-29 to BM-30; and Ashley, 132.

187. Orlov, 112-115; and Miller, 71-72.

188. Orlov, 113; and Ottis, 95.

189. Ottis, 94-95, 112-114.

190. Molnar, et. al., 51; and *Al Qaeda Manual*, BM-30.

191. Ottis, 92-98; Molnar, et. al., 80; and Miller, 71-72.

192. Orlov, 152.

193. Ibid., 151-153; *Al Qaeda Manual*, BM-29 to BM-30; and Ottis, 98.

194. Orlov, 112-113.

195. Ibid.

196. Ottis, 113-114.

197. Prikhodko, 19.

198. Ibid; Miller, 71-72.

199. Ibid., 3, 37-41, 81, 129.

200. Orlov, 112; Also see Ottis, 114. Ottis provides an example of a failed meeting where minimal security measures were taken and resulted in the capture of the network leader.

201. Ashley, 233.

202. *Al Qaeda Manual*, BM-60 to BM-65.

203. Ibid., 119; and *Al Qaeda Manual*, BM-34.

204. For examples of recognition and safe signals, see Prikhodko, 18; and Orlov, 112-114.

205. Ibid., 115-116.

206. Ottis, 110-113, 133, 174.

207. Byman, 17-18.

208. Orlov, 112-115, 151-153.

209. For example, Sageman notes, "Evolution of the three main clusters [al-Qaeda and its associated movements or the "Global Salafi Jihad," per Sageman] followed a pattern of growth through friendship, kinship, worship, and discipleship." Sageman, *Understanding*, 50; in this sense, the links outside friends and family when

the movement begins are not the same as active recruiting that takes place at locations of religious "worship," and "discipleship" may be mistaken for part of the recruiting process, where the recruiter identifies, targets, befriends, and then disciples to a potential recruit prior to actually recruiting them.

210. DA PAM 550-104, 7.

211. As 550-104 explains, "underground recruitment techniques are probably most successful when selectively applied."DA PAM 550-104, 119; and Lindsay Moran, *Blowing My Cover: My life as a CIA Spy*, (New York, NY: Penguin Group, 2005), 33; also, *Al Qaeda Manual*, BM-15 to BM-16; under "Necessary Qualifications [for] the Organization's members."

212. DA PAM 550-104, 111-119.

213. Former Central Intelligence Agency case officer, Lindsay Moran, refers this process as the "recruiting cycle," consisting of the following steps, "spot, assess, develop, and recruit." Lindsay Moran, *Blowing My Cover: My life as a CIA Spy*, (New York, NY: Penguin Group, 2005), 33, 34; Sageman, *Understanding*, 122; Sageman refers to the same cycle; Buchanan 42-47. Buchanan uses weak links within social networking circles to show how weak links bridge strong link networks, this same idea applies to clandestine recruiting. In this case, the recruiter may have been given the name of a potential recruit or identified a potential recruit, then found an acquaintance of both the possible recruit and recruiter to introduce the two so as not to draw attention to the recruiter.

214. See Sageman, *Understanding*, 142-143; for example, jihadi networks throughout the world have recruiters at local Mosques that can identify potential recruits, go through the recruitment process, and recruit these individuals if they are assessed to have leadership potential. Others with little long-term potential are provided instructions to get to the area of conflict and will be either foot soldiers, or martyred. For example, see Cordesman, *Iraq's Sunni Insurgents*, 2; *Al Qaeda Manual*, BM-93 to BM-98; provides detailed instructions on recruiting, including a recruiting cycle. An example of the type of individual that is good at clandestine recruiting is the "catalyst" from Brafman and Beckstrom, 120-129. Brafman and Beckstrom describe the "catalyst" as someone who are naturally inquisitive and interested in others, who like to meet new people, and all the while, are "mapping" them to determine their potential as members of the network. Brafman and Beckstrom's "catalyst" attributes all apply to the clandestine recruiter, despite their inherent business and social networking application in *The Starfish and the Spider*. Another possible location for identifying and approaching potential recruits is the counterinsurgent detention facilities. As Bob Woodward quotes a Defense Intelligence Agency report, "'Insurgent recruiters...exploit [detained individual's] feelings of humiliation, anger and fear to entice them to join the insurgency while in coalition custody or immediately after release;" Woodward, 35.

215. DA PAM 550-104, 119.

216. Orlov, 93-95.

217. Robert Windrem notes, "In some cases, al-Qaida security personnel have married into local tribes and clans, making them part of the extended family and giving Bin Laden and others additional protection." Robert Windrem, "Where is Osama Bin Laden? An analysis," *Deep Backgound: NBC News Investigates*, (June 13, 2008), under title, http://deepbackground.msnbc.msn.com/archive/2008/06/13/ 1138296. aspx [accessed January 22, 2009].

218. Dr. Charles P.Neimeyer and Major General James N. Mattis, "Interview 1: Preparing for Counterinsurgency," in *Al-Anbar Awakening: Volume 1, American Perspectives, U.S. Marines and Counterinsurgency in Iraq 2004-2009*, (Quantico, Virginia: Marine Corps University Press, 2009) http://www.marines.mil/unit/ hqmc/Documents/historical/Al-AnbarAwakeningVolI.pdf. [accessed October 20, 2011], 33-34.

219. Bern, 109-110; and Miller, 98.

220. Ibid., 109-113.

221. Ibid., 112-113.

222. Author's experience in Iraq and Kosovo.

223. Bern, 110-111; and Ottis, 58-59.

224. DA PAM 550-104, 223.

225. Bern, 110-111.

226. Ibid., 110-111.

227. Ibid., 111; and DA PAM 550-104, 222-226.

228. Ottis, 41-43.

229. Ibid., 113-114.

230. DA PAM 550-104, 209; and *Al Qaeda Manual*, BM-57 to BM-58.

231. DA PAM 550-104, 209; an example from 550-104, used by the Huks in the Philippines, "If government troops approached a village and a man chopping wood observed them, he would increase the rate of his swing. A woman noticing his increased pace would place a white and blue dress side-by-side on the clothesline. Other members of the security net would pass the warning on that a government patrol was in the area."

232. Bern, 113-114.

233. Ibid., 127-139.

234. Simon West, Mike Stenson, Chad Oman, and Branko Lustig, "Scene 5," *Black Hawk Down*, DVD, directed by Ridley Scott, (Culver City, CA: Columbia Pictures, 2002).

235. Ney notes, "Personal security is of such primal necessity—that it must be continually and continuously checked and inspected by the resistance members. Even the slightest slip of security must be corrected drastically and on the spot by the members observing it." Ney, 155; and Prikhodko, 33.

236. Prikhodko, 34.

237. Lindsay Moran, *Blowing My Cover: My life as a CIA Spy*, (New York, NY: Penguin Group, 2005), 206-207.

238. Skills may also be transferred under from one organization to another in counterinsurgent detention facilities. As author Bob Woodward directly quotes from a Defense Intelligence Agency report, "'Insurgents and terrorists use coalition detention facilities to trade information on successful tactics and techniques, teach detainees insurgent and terrorist skills, preach radical Islam and recruit new members into the insurgency;'" Woodward, 34.

239. Prikhodko, 33.

240. DA PAM 550-104, 121.

241. Jafarzadeh, 108.

242. Burton.

243. Gordon and Trainor, 492.

244. Julian E. Barnes, "Cracking an Insurgent Cell," *U.S. News & World Report* (January 9, 2006), 44. Barnes report highlights the motivation of some insurgent recruits, "'I have six brothers...I have to support my family—that is why I did what I did.'" When the cell leader is captured, he explains why he took the leadership role, and in doing so shows how revenge drives many to insurgency and thus, care must be taken not to produce more insurgents than are killed or captured, "The reason I did this is that five from my family got killed by the Americans." As Chehab notes, "[the insurgent leader] replied that recruitment was easy because people were upset by the inappropriate way American soldiers searched people's homes." Chehab, 21.

245. "There were few jobs. For $50 or $100, groups could hire local Iraqis to take a shot at the Americans." Michael R. Gordon and Bernard E. Trainor, *Cobra II: The Inside Story of the Invasion and Occupation of Iraq*, (New York, NY: Pantheon Books, 2006), 492.

246. This illustrates the analogy that low hanging fruit may be nothing more than a security buffer between the more important cells.

247. DA PAM 550-104, 15.

248. See FM 3-24, 1-17, 1-19 to 1-20; *U.S. Government Counterinsurgency Guide*, (Washington, D.C.: Bureau of Political-Military Affairs, 2009), www.state.gov/t/pm/ppa/pmppt [accessed March 25, 2009], 26.

249. "The object of war is specifically 'to preserve oneself and destroy the enemy;'" Mao Tse-Tung, *On the Protracted War*, (Peking, China: Foreign Languages Press, 1967), 61-63; 61; and McCuen, 51-52.

250. McCuen explains, "more important from the revolutionary point of view is that a primary objective is preservation of the revolutionary forces. As long as these forces exist in some form, the governing power must conduct expensive and tiring operations." McCuen, 51.

251. Sir Robert Thompson referred to this as "the famous 'one step backwards'" for insurgent movements, and noted, "When facing defeat, both militarily and

politically...it [may] be considerably more than one step." Thompson, 43; also, "The element of duration makes a vast difference in the intrinsic structure of an underground movement. If for example, it is based on the assumption of a protracted war, then the entire plan and strategy must be radically different from one organized for a short term only;" Jan Karski, *The Story of a Secret State*, (Boston: Houghton, Mifflin Co., 1944), 231, as quoted in Ney, 46.

252. FM 3-24, 1-6 to 1- 8.

253. Ibid., 1-5.

254. Ibid.

255. Naveh, 5.

256. Ibid., 6.

257. Henry Butterfield notes, "The Kremlin had long entertained misgivings about Havana's strident views of revolution, its determination that the job of revolutionaries was to make revolution and not wait for favorable conditions." Henry Butterfield Ryan, *The Fall of Che Guevara: A Story of Soldiers, Spies, and Diplomats*, (New York, NY: Oxford University Press, 1998), 61.

258. As Moran explains the pressures of working as a CIA case officer, "*I've been doing this spying thing for months now, and I've realized: You can never be one hundred percent sure [you are not being survielled]. Still, my eyes are trained to dart around at all times, even when I am doing everyday errands or just out for a walk. I'm constantly on the lookout, and on a night like tonight, all my senses are on high alert. I feel less like a predator and prey. Truth be told, I am almost always terrified of getting caught.*" Lindsay Moran, *Blowing My Cover: My life as a CIA Spy*, (New York, NY: Penguin Group, 2005), 186.

259. As Orlov notes, "In the life of an underground operative nothing is as simple as it is in the lives of ordinary, carefree people." Orlov, 110; also see Foot, 163; and Sageman, *Understanding*, 132.

260. Momboisse, 64.

261. As Moran highlights her fear for her agents, "I was on the lookout all the time. *Am I being followed? Is someone following one of my agents? Is my phone tapped? Is my house bugged? Where would they have planted the video cameras? What if I get arrested? Worse yet, what if one of my agents gets arrested?*" Lindsay Moran, *Blowing My Cover: My life as a CIA Spy*, (New York, NY: Penguin Group, 2005), 198-199.

262. Kyle B. Teamey, "Arresting Insurgency," *Joint Forces Quarterly*, no. 47 (4th quarter 2007): 118, http://www.ndu.edu/inss/Press/jfq_pages/editions/i47/27.pdf [accessed March 5, 2009]; Woodward, 35. Quoting a Defense Intelligence Agency (DIA) report, Woodward highlights this issue, "insurgents, terrorists, foreign fighters and insurgent leaders captured and released by coalition forces may be more dangerous than they were before being detained."

263. Author's experience with detainees in Iraq. When expected patterns of detention changed the detainees would become visibly upset, such as additional days at one

detention facility before moving to the next level of detention. Although these delays were caused by routine issues such as lack of aircraft or weather delays, the detainees were not aware of the nature of the delay. The expected pattern was so well known that when it was deviated from, the detainees became nervous at the idea that something unexpected would happen.

264. John McLaughlin, "Questions and Answers Highlights" transcript, in *Unrestricted Warfare Symposium 2008*, ed. Ronald R. Luman, (Laurel, MD: John Hopkins University of Applied Physics Laboratory, 2008), 130.

265. Author's figure.

266. Naveh, 5.

267. Molnar, et. al., 6,51.

268. Audiences and interaction based on Dr. Gordon McCormick's "Diamond Model"; see Eric P. Wendt, "Strategic Counterinsurgency Modeling," *Special Warfare* (September 2005), 5.

269. Otis, 89.

270. So for example, the combined U.S. and Northern Alliance forces soundly defeated the Taliban's overt fighting force in Afghanistan by December of 2001. Yet, as the Taliban transferred from the "government" of Afghanistan to the insurgent fighting against a US- and NATO-backed Afghan government, over time, the Taliban has rebuilt its overt forces. This growth was based on the efforts of the elements that survived and went underground. They simply faded into the population or crossed the border to sanctuary areas in Pakistan. From 2006 to 2009, the Taliban's overt force has been reconstituted, and transitioned from the latent-insipient phase to the guerrilla warfare phase. In some areas, the Taliban has been successful enough to even transition from the guerrilla warfare phase to the war-of-movement phase where the Taliban controls areas in Afghanistan and conduct large-scale combat operations. Yet, even if all of the Taliban's overt fighting force was defeated today, the Taliban would simply regress back to the latent-incipient phase, and reorganize and rebuild based on the clandestine cellular network that survived.

271. FM 3-24, 1-29.

272. Trinquier, 8-9.

273. D. Jones, *Ending the Debate*, 166.

274. Ibid., 165-166.

275. Ibid.

www.ingramcontent.com/pod-product-compliance
Lightning Source LLC
Chambersburg PA
CBHW060412290526
45791CB00002B/721